I0020679

Clojure for Java Developers

Transition smoothly from Java to the most widely used
functional JVM-based language – Clojure

Eduardo Díaz

[PACKT] open source *
PUBLISHING   community experience distilled

BIRMINGHAM - MUMBAI

Clojure for Java Developers

Copyright © 2016 Packt Publishing

All rights reserved. No part of this book may be reproduced, stored in a retrieval system, or transmitted in any form or by any means, without the prior written permission of the publisher, except in the case of brief quotations embedded in critical articles or reviews.

Every effort has been made in the preparation of this book to ensure the accuracy of the information presented. However, the information contained in this book is sold without warranty, either express or implied. Neither the author, nor Packt Publishing, and its dealers and distributors will be held liable for any damages caused or alleged to be caused directly or indirectly by this book.

Packt Publishing has endeavored to provide trademark information about all of the companies and products mentioned in this book by the appropriate use of capitals. However, Packt Publishing cannot guarantee the accuracy of this information.

First published: February 2016

Production reference: 1190216

Published by Packt Publishing Ltd.
Livery Place
35 Livery Street
Birmingham B3 2PB, UK.

ISBN 978-1-78528-150-1

www.packtpub.com

Credits

Author
Eduardo Díaz

Reviewers
Ning Sun

Nate West

Commissioning Editor
Kunal Parikh

Acquisition Editor
Usha Iyer

Content Development Editors
Neeshma Ramakrishnan

Kajal Thapar

Technical Editor
Saurabh Malhotra

Copy Editor
Sneha Singh

Project Coordinator
Shweta H. Birwatkar

Proofreaders
Safis Editing

Indexer
Hemangini Bari

Production Coordinator
Shantanu N. Zagade

Cover Work
Shantanu N. Zagade

About the Author

Eduardo Díaz is a developer with a strong background in the Java language. He has a passion for functional programming and new programming paradigms. His work includes full stack development, systems design, and high volume real time data processing.

He has worked on every technology related problem you can imagine, as a consultant solving anything related to Java, UNIX, C, or any other strange problem you might have had.

As a developer, he has been working for around 10 years on Java, Python, Scala, Clojure, in the media, bank, and primarily communications industries.

He is currently working at Grupo Expansion, a media company, where he helps design and implement a new content delivery platform aiming to empower content editors and encourage developers to find new ways to use data.

First of all, I would like to thank Neeshma Ramakrishnan and Kajal Thapar at Packt Publishing, they are the best editors, they have an incredible amount of patience and without them, there would be nothing even close to a book.

I would also like to thank my colleagues and friends at Grupo Expansion, Lucasian Labs, and Javanes; they have helped me grow in every way imaginable. Thanks for everything!

Last but not the least, thanks to my family for always keeping up with me, cheering me up, believing in me and helping in everything I do, even when it means not seeing me for weeks or months. I truly value your support!

About the Reviewer

Ning Sun is a software engineer currently working for a China-based startup, LeanCloud, providing one-stop "backend as a service" for mobile apps. Being a startup engineer, he has to solve various kinds of problems and play different kinds of roles; however, he has always been an enthusiast for open source technology. He contributes to several open source projects and has also learned a lot from them.

At LeanCloud, he built a messaging system that supports tens of millions of clients per day. The system is fully powered by Clojure and its ecosystem. He has been an early member of Clojure Chinese community since 2011. He has delivered talks at several meetups and has been very active in the mailing list and open source projects. Ning created Clojure RPC library "Slacker", which is widely used at LeanCloud and several other companies.

He worked on `https://Delicious.com` in 2013, which is known as one of the most important websites in the early Web 2.0 era.

He has been a reviewer of two books about Solr at Packt Publishing. Also, he was the reviewer of *Programming Clojure*, Chinese edition.

You can always find him on `Github.com/sunng87` and `Twitter.com/Sunng`.

www.PacktPub.com

eBooks, discount offers, and more

Did you know that Packt offers eBook versions of every book published, with PDF and ePub files available? You can upgrade to the eBook version at www.PacktPub.com and as a print book customer, you are entitled to a discount on the eBook copy. Get in touch with us at customercare@packtpub.com for more details.

At www.PacktPub.com, you can also read a collection of free technical articles, sign up for a range of free newsletters and receive exclusive discounts and offers on Packt books and eBooks.

https://www2.packtpub.com/books/subscription/packtlib

Do you need instant solutions to your IT questions? PacktLib is Packt's online digital book library. Here, you can search, access, and read Packt's entire library of books.

Why subscribe?

- Fully searchable across every book published by Packt
- Copy and paste, print, and bookmark content
- On demand and accessible via a web browser

Table of Contents

Preface

In the last few years, we have seen a widespread tendency to create new languages for JVM. There are all sorts of new languages with different paradigms and different ways of working.

Clojure is one of those languages, one that we believe is worth learning.

Over the course of this book, you will learn about Clojure and how opinionated it is. You will learn why immutable objects are not only possible, but it is a good idea to use them.

You will learn about functional programming and see how it fits the concept of immutable programs.

You will understand the very powerful idea of representing your code as a data structure of the same language.

It is important to note that we will build all this knowledge on top of what you already know; this book assumes that you understand the Java language and a bit of how it works. It assumes that you understand how to create classes and objects, how to call methods, and also a bit about the JVM. We will find similarities and differences from the Java language that you already know, so you can understand how the Clojure world works.

It is said that a great programmer is not the one who knows a lot of different programming languages, it is someone who knows different programming paradigms.

Clojure brings ideas from Lisp and functional programming, which are different to what you are used to. This book will help you understand the power behind these ideas and why a language so old still exists and has a place.

Learning Lisp is one of the great pleasures of life, I hope you enjoy it!

What this book covers

Chapter 1, Getting Started with Clojure, is your first step with Clojure, from how to install an interpreter, how to use the IntelliJ plugin Cursive Clojure, and how to start writing your first lines of code in Clojure.

Chapter 2, Namespaces, Packages, and Tests, deals with how every other language needs a way to organize our code. We do it with namespaces, and we start learning by doing little experiments and by comparing with the Java packages we already know.

Chapter 3, Interacting with Java, discusses the fact that one of the most useful features of Clojure is that it can be hosted on top of other platforms. Java is probably one of the most common platforms, and here we learn how to interact with Java code and libraries and how to expose our Clojure code to Java.

Chapter 4, Collections and Functional Programming, tells us that functional programming and immutable data structures (or collections) are fundamental to programming in the Clojure language; here we understand how we can write meaningful programs using immutable data structures and how functional programming is ideal for that.

Chapter 5, Multimethods and Protocols, introduces new tools and ideas of Clojure that help you write much more flexible and simple codes. Destructuring allows you to gain instant access to the data you need from a data structure. Multimethods and protocols are similar to Java's polymorphism but give you a whole new level of flexibility that you could only dream about.

Chapter 6, Concurrency, tells us about how in the modern world concurrency plays an extremely important part. This chapter also tells us about Clojure's native primitives for concurrency and again you will learn why immutable data structures are a great ally when writing concurrent programs.

Chapter 7, Macros in Clojure, deals with the fact that these are not the Excel macros you are used to, they are a way in which you can modify your program's source code at compile time. This is one of Lisp's big ideas and one that gives you immense flexibility. Here we understand a little of how to use this feature.

What you need for this book

You need the Java 8 SDK.

You should be able to run samples on any OS; our samples should be easier to follow in environments where there is a shell available. (We focus mainly on Mac OS X.)

Who this book is for

This book is for developers who are familiar with Java and the JVM.

Ideally, you know how the classloader works, how to generate JAR files and consume them; you are familiar with Java's most common libraries and classes.

If you are not familiar with this, you will be able to follow this book but you won't get the most from the comparisons and samples.

Conventions

In this book, you will find a number of text styles that distinguish between different kinds of information. Here are some examples of these styles and an explanation of their meaning.

Code words in text, database table names, folder names, filenames, file extensions, pathnames, dummy URLs, user input, and Twitter handles are shown as follows: "We are using `:require` to include functions from the `clojure.test` and the `ns-playground.core` packages."

A block of code is set as follows:

```
curl -O https://raw.githubusercontent.com/technomancy/leiningen/stable/bin/lein
# The next step just set up the lein script in your path, you can do it any way you wish
mv lein ~/bin
echo "export PATH=$PATH:~/bin/">> ~/.bashrc
source ~/.bashrc
# Everything should be running now, let's test it
lein help
```

When we wish to draw your attention to a particular part of a code block, the relevant lines or items are set in bold:

```
lein new app getting-started
cd getting-started
lein run
# Hello, world!
```

Any command-line input or output is written as follows:

```
lein uberjar
```

New terms and **important words** are shown in bold. Words that you see on the screen, for example, in menus or dialog boxes, appear in the text like this: "After that you can run any tests, just open your test file and go to **Tools | Run Tests** in the current NS in REPL."

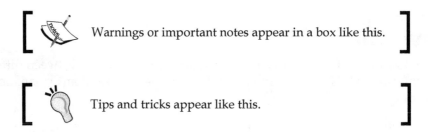

Warnings or important notes appear in a box like this.

Tips and tricks appear like this.

Reader feedback

Feedback from our readers is always welcome. Let us know what you think about this book—what you liked or disliked. Reader feedback is important for us as it helps us develop titles that you will really get the most out of.

To send us general feedback, simply e-mail feedback@packtpub.com, and mention the book's title in the subject of your message.

If there is a topic that you have expertise in and you are interested in either writing or contributing to a book, see our author guide at www.packtpub.com/authors.

Customer support

Now that you are the proud owner of a Packt book, we have a number of things to help you to get the most from your purchase.

Downloading the example code

You can download the example code files from your account at http://www.packtpub.com for all the Packt Publishing books you have purchased. If you purchased this book elsewhere, you can visit http://www.packtpub.com/support and register to have the files e-mailed directly to you.

Downloading the color images of this book

We also provide you with a PDF file that has color images of the screenshots/ diagrams used in this book. The color images will help you better understand the changes in the output. You can download this file from `https://www.` `packtpub.com/sites/default/files/downloads/ClojureforJavaDevelopers_` `ColorImages.pdf`.

Errata

Although we have taken every care to ensure the accuracy of our content, mistakes do happen. If you find a mistake in one of our books—maybe a mistake in the text or the code—we would be grateful if you could report this to us. By doing so, you can save other readers from frustration and help us improve subsequent versions of this book. If you find any errata, please report them by visiting `http://www.packtpub.` `com/submit-errata`, selecting your book, clicking on the **Errata Submission Form** link, and entering the details of your errata. Once your errata are verified, your submission will be accepted and the errata will be uploaded to our website or added to any list of existing errata under the Errata section of that title.

To view the previously submitted errata, go to `https://www.packtpub.com/books/` `content/support` and enter the name of the book in the search field. The required information will appear under the **Errata** section.

Piracy

Piracy of copyrighted material on the Internet is an ongoing problem across all media. At Packt, we take the protection of our copyright and licenses very seriously. If you come across any illegal copies of our works in any form on the Internet, please provide us with the location address or website name immediately so that we can pursue a remedy.

Please contact us at `copyright@packtpub.com` with a link to the suspected pirated material.

We appreciate your help in protecting our authors and our ability to bring you valuable content.

Questions

If you have a problem with any aspect of this book, you can contact us at `questions@packtpub.com`, and we will do our best to address the problem.

1
Getting Started with Clojure

Welcome to the world of Clojure! If you are here, you probably know a little about Lisp or Clojure, but you don't really have an idea of how things work in this world.

We will get to know Clojure by comparing each feature to what you already know from Java. You will see that there are lists, maps and sets just like in Java, but they are immutable. To work with these kinds of collections, you need a different approach; a different paradigm.

This is what we will try to accomplish in this book, to give you a different way to approach problems. We hope you end up using Clojure in your every day life, but if you don't, we hope you use a new approach toward problem solving.

In this chapter, we will cover the following topics:

- Getting to know Clojure
- Installing Leiningen
- Using a **Read Eval Print Loop (REPL)**
- Installing and using Cursive Clojure
- Clojure's simple syntax
- Clojure's data types and their relationship to the JVM's data types
- Special syntax for functions

Getting to know Clojure

Before getting started with Clojure, you should know some of its features and what it shares with Java.

Clojure is a programming language that inherits a lot of characteristics from Lisp. You might think of Lisp as that weird programming language with all the parentheses. You need to keep in mind that Clojure chooses to embrace functional programming. This makes it very different from current mainstream programming languages. You will get to know about immutable data structures and how to write programs without changing variable values.

You will also find that Clojure is a dynamic programming language, which makes it a little easier and faster to write programs than using statically typed languages. There is also the concept of using a REPL, a tool that allows you to connect to a program running environment and change code dynamically. It is a very powerful tool.

At last, you will find out that you can convert Clojure to anything you like. You can create or use a statically typed system and bend the language to become what you like. A good example of this is the `core.typed` library, which allows you to specify the type information without adding support to the compiler.

Installing Leiningen

We are used to having certain tools to help us build our code, such as Ant, Maven, and Gradle.

In the Clojure ecosystem, the de facto standard for dependency and build management is Leiningen (affectionately named after the short story "Leiningen versus the Ants", which I recommend reading at `http://en.wikipedia.org/wiki/Leiningen_Versus_the_Ants`); Leiningen strives to be a familiar to Java developers, it gets the best ideas from Maven, like: convention over configuration. It also gets ideas from Ant like custom scripting and plugins.

Installing it is very simple, let's check how to do it on Mac OS X (installing on Linux should be the same) using bash as your default shell.

You should also have Java 7 or 8 already installed and configured in your path.

You can check the detailed instructions on the Leiningen project page
`http://leiningen.org/`. If you want to get a Leiningen installation up
and running, this is what you would have to do:

```
curl -O https://raw.githubusercontent.com/technomancy/leiningen/stable/
bin/lein

# The next step just set up the lein script in your path, you can do it
any way you wish

mv lein ~/bin

echo "export PATH=$PATH:~/bin/">> ~/.bashrc

source ~/.bashrc

# Everything should be running now, let's test it

lein help
```

The first time you run the `lein` command, it downloads everything needed from the
internet. This makes it very easy to distribute your code, you can even include the
`lein` script with your own projects and make it easier for other developers to get up
and running, the only real requirement is the JDK.

Using a REPL

One of the main advantages of Clojure (and Lisp) is interactive development, the
REPL is the base of what can be achieved with interactive programming, it allows
you to connect to a running VM running Clojure and execute or modify code on
the fly.

There is a story about how NASA was able to debug and correct a bug on a $100
million piece of hardware that was 100 million miles away (`http://www.flownet.
com/gat/jpl-lisp.html`).

We have that same power with Clojure and Leiningen and invoking it is very simple,
you just need a single command:

```
lein repl
```

This is what you'll get after running the preceding command:

```
● ● ●                    ⬆ iamedu — lein repl — lein — java

# iamedu at Eduardos-MacBook-Pro.local in ~ [4:18:18]
$ lein repl
nREPL server started on port 55995 on host 127.0.0.1 - nrepl://127.0.0.1:55995
REPL-y 0.3.5, nREPL 0.2.6
Clojure 1.6.0
Java HotSpot(TM) 64-Bit Server VM 1.8.0_25-b17
    Docs: (doc function-name-here)
          (find-doc "part-of-name-here")
  Source: (source function-name-here)
 Javadoc: (javadoc java-object-or-class-here)
    Exit: Control+D or (exit) or (quit)
 Results: Stored in vars *1, *2, *3, an exception in *e

user=>
```

Let's go into a bit more detail, as we can see we are running with the following programs:

- Java 8
- Clojure 1.6.0

We can also get some nice suggestions on how to see documentation, source, Javadoc, and previous errors.

The nREPL protocol

One particular thing that is important to note is the nREPL protocol; Someday it might grant us the power to go into a machine running 100 million miles away.

When you fire up your REPL, the first thing you see is:

```
nREPL server started on port 55995 on host 127.0.0.1 -
nrepl://127.0.0.1:55995
REPL-y 0.3.5, nREPL 0.2.6
```

What it is saying is that there's a Clojure process running an nREPL server on port 55995. We have connected to it using a very simple client that allows us to interact with the Clojure process.

The really interesting bit is that you can connect to a remote host just as easily; let's try attaching an REPL to the same process by simply typing the following command:

```
lein repl :connect localhost:55995
```

Most IDEs have a good integration with Clojure and most of them use this exact mechanism, as clients that work a little more intelligently.

Hello world

Now that we are inside the REPL, (any of the two) let's try writing our first expression, go on and type:

```
"Hello world"
```

You should get back a value from the REPL saying `Hello world`, this is not really a program, and it is the `Hello world` value printed back by the print phase of the REPL.

Let's now try to write our first Lisp form:

```
(println "Hello world")
```

This first expression looks different from what we are used to, it is called an S-expression and it is the standard Lisp way.

There are a couple of things to remember with S-expressions:

- They are lists (hence, the name, Lisp)
- The first element of the list is the action that we want to execute, the rest are the parameters of that action (one two three).

So we are asking for the string Hello world to be printed, but if we look a bit closer at the output, as shown in the following screenshot, there is a nil that we weren't expecting:

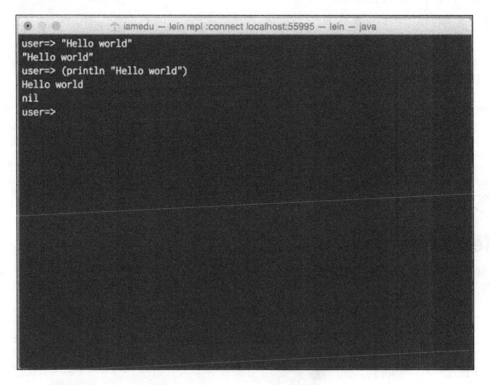

The reason for this is that the println function returns the value nil (Clojure's equivalent for null) after printing Hello world.

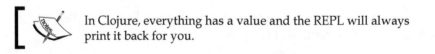 In Clojure, everything has a value and the REPL will always print it back for you.

REPL utilities and conventions

As we saw, the Leiningen nREPL client prints help text; but how does that work? Let's explore some of the other utilities that we have.

Try each of them to get a feeling of what it does with the help of the following table:

Function	Description	Sample
doc	Prints out a function's docstring	(doc println)
source	Prints a function's source code, it must be written in Clojure	(source println)
javadoc	Open the javadoc for a class in the browser	(javadoc java.lang. Integer)

Let's check how these functions work:

```
user=> (javadoc java.util.List)
;; Should open the javadoc for java.util.List


user=> (doc doc)
-------------------------
clojure.repl/doc
([name])
Macro
  Prints documentation for a var or special form given its name
nil


user=> (source doc)
(defmacro doc
"Prints documentation for a var or special form given its name"
  {:added "1.0"}
  [name]
  (if-let [special-name ('{& fn catch try finally try} name)]
    (#'print-doc (#'special-doc special-name))
    (cond
      (special-doc-map name) `(#'print-doc (#'special-doc '~name))
      (find-ns name) `(#'print-doc (#'namespace-doc (find-ns '~name)))
      (resolve name) `(#'print-doc (meta (var ~name))))))
nil
```

Downloading the example code

You can download the example code files from your account at http://www.packtpub.com for all the Packt Publishing books you have purchased. If you purchased this book elsewhere, you can visit http://www.packtpub.com/support and register to have the files e-mailed directly to you.

What you are seeing here is metadata pertaining to the doc function; Clojure has the ability to store metadata about every function or var you use. Most of the Clojure core functions include a doc string and the source of the function and this is something that will become very handy in your day to day work.

Besides these functions, we also get easy access to the latest three values and the latest exceptions that happened in the REPL, let's check this out:

```
user=> 2
2
user=> 3
3
user=> 4
4
user=> (* *1 *2 *3) ;; We are multiplying over here the last three
values
24 ;;We get 24!
user=> (/ 1 0) ;; Let's try dividing by zero
ArithmeticException Divide by zero clojure.lang.Numbers.divide
(Numbers.java:156)
user=> *e
#<ArithmeticException java.lang.ArithmeticException: Divide by zero>

user=> (.getMessage *e)
"Divide by zero"
```

 *e gives you access to the actual plain old Java exception object, so you can analyze and introspect it at runtime.

You can imagine the possibilities of being able to execute and introspect code with this, but what about the tools that we are already used to? How can we use this with an IDE?

Let's check now how to create a new Clojure project, we'll use Leiningen from the command line to understand what is happening.

Creating a new project

Leiningen can help us create a new project using templates, there is a wide variety of templates available and you can build and distribute your own in Maven.

Some of the most common types of templates are:

- Creating a `jar` library (the default template)
- Creating a command-line app
- Creating a Clojure web app

Let's create a new Clojure command-line app and run it:

```
lein new app getting-started
cd getting-started
lein run
# Hello, world!
```

Project structure

Leiningen is similar to other Java development tools; it uses a similar convention and allows for heavy customizations in the `project.clj` file.

If you are familiar with Maven or Gradle, you can think of it as `pom.xml` or `build.gradle` respectively.

The following screenshot is the project structure:

```
# iamedu at Eduardos-MacBook-Pro.local in ~/Development/getting-started [20:47:2
3]
$ tree .
.
├── LICENSE
├── README.md
├── doc
│   └── intro.md
├── project.clj
├── resources
├── src
│   └── getting_started
│       └── core.clj
└── test
    └── getting_started
        └── core_test.clj

6 directories, 6 files

# iamedu at Eduardos-MacBook-Pro.local in ~/Development/getting-started [20:47:2
3]
$ |
```

As you can see in the preceding screenshot, there are four main folders:

- `resources`: It holds everything that should be in the class path, such as files, images, configuration files, properties files, and other resources needed at runtime.

- `src`: Your Clojure source files; they are ordered in a very similar fashion to the `classpath`.

- `dev-resources`: Everything that should be in the `classpath` in development (when you are running Leiningen). You can override your "production" files here and add files that are needed for tests to run.

- `test`: Your tests; this code doesn't get packaged but it is run every time you execute the Leiningen test.

Creating a standalone app

Once your project is created, you can build and run a Java standalone command-line app quite easily, let's try it now:

```
lein uberjar
java -jar target/uberjar/getting-started-0.1.0-SNAPSHOT-standalone.jar
# Hello, World!
```

As you can see, it is quite easy to create a standalone app and it is very similar to using Maven or Gradle.

Using Cursive Clojure

Java already has some great tools to help us be more productive and write higher quality code and we don't need to forget about those tools. There are several plugins for Clojure depending on what your IDE is. Have a look at them from the following table:

IDE	Plugins
IntelliJ	Cursive Clojure, La Clojure
NetBeans	NetBeans Clojure (works with NetBeans 7.4)
Eclipse	CounterClockwise
Emacs	Cider
VIM	vim-fireplace, vim-leiningen

A lot of people writing real Clojure code use Emacs and I actually like using vim as my main development tool, but don't worry, our main IDE will be IntelliJ + Cursive Clojure throughout the book.

Installing Cursive Clojure

You can check the full documentation for Cursive at their website (`https://cursiveclojure.com/`), it is still under development but it is quite stable and a great aid when writing Clojure code.

We are going to use the latest IntelliJ Community Edition release, which at the time of this writing is version 14.

You can download IntelliJ from here `https://www.jetbrains.com/idea/download/`.

Installing Cursive Clojure is very simple, you need to add a repository for IntelliJ. You'll find the instructions to your specific IntelliJ version here: `https://cursiveclojure.com/userguide/`.

After you have installed Cursive Clojure, we are ready to go.

Now, we are ready to import our getting started project into Cursive Clojure.

 Cursive Clojure doesn't currently have support to create Leiningen projects from within the IDE; however, support is great in order to import them.

Here is how you will do it:

1. Click on **File**.
2. Import project.
3. Look for your project.
4. Open the folder or the `project.clj` file.
5. Follow the **Next** steps in the IDE.

Now, we are ready to go, you can use the Cursive Clojure as your main development tool. There are a few more things to do with your IDE but I recommend you to look for them; they are important and will come in handy:

- To know how to execute the project
- To know how to execute the tests
- To open an REPL connected to some project.
- The key binding to execute some given piece of code (run form before cursor in REPL)
- The key binding to execute a given file (load file in REPL)

One important part of Clojure programming is that it can modify and reevaluate code in runtime. Check the manual of your current version of Clojure and check for the structural editing section (`https://cursiveclojure.com/userguide/paredit.html`). It is one of the most useful functionalities of Clojure IDEs and a direct consequence of the Clojure syntax.

I recommend you to check other functionalities from the manual. I really recommend checking the Cursive Clojure manual, it includes animations of how each functionality works.

You will use the last two key bindings quite a lot, so it is important to set them up correctly. There is more information about keybindings at `https://cursiveclojure.com/userguide/keybindings.html`.

Getting started with Clojure code and data

Let's take a deep dive into Clojure's syntax now, it is pretty different from other languages but it is actually much simpler. Lisps have a very regular syntax, with few special rules. As we said earlier, Clojure code is made of S-expressions and S-expressions are just lists. Let's look at some examples of lists to become familiar with lists in Lisp.

```
(1 2 3 4)
(println "Hello world")
(one two three)
("one" two three)
```

All of the above are lists, but not all of them are valid code. Remember, only lists where the first element is a function can be considered valid expressions. So, here only the following could be valid expressions:

```
(println "Hello world")
(one two three)
```

If println and one are defined as functions.

Let's see a piece of Clojure code, to finally explain how everything works.

```
(defn some-function [times parameter]
"Prints a string certain number of times"
  (dotimes [x times]
    (println parameter)))
```

Lists in Clojure

Clojure is based around "forms" or lists. In Clojure, same as every Lisp, the way to denote a list is with parentheses, so here are some examples of lists in the last code:

```
(println parameter)
(dotimes [x times] (println parameter))
(defn some-function [times parameter] (dotimes [x times] (println
parameter)))
```

Lists are one data type in Clojure and they are also the way to express code; you will learn later about all the benefits of expressing code as data. The first one is that it is really simple, anything you can do must be expressed as a list! Let's look at some other examples of executable code:

```
(* 1 2 3)
(+ 5 9 7)
(/ 4 5)
(- 2 3 4)
(map inc [1 2 3 4 5 6])
```

I encourage you to write everything into the REPL, so you get a good notion of what's happening.

Operations in Clojure

In Clojure, MOST of the executable forms have this structure:

```
(op parameter-1parameter-2 ....)
```

op is the operation to be executed followed by all the parameters it needs, let's analyze each of our previous forms in this new light:

```
(+ 1 2 3)
```

We are asking to execute the + (addition) operation with the parameters 1, 2, and 3. The expected result is 6.

Let's analyze something a bit more complicated:

```
(map inc [1 2 3 4 5 6])
```

In this, we are asking to execute the clojure.core/map function with two parameters:

- inc is a function name, it takes a number and increments it
- [1 2 3 4 5 6] is a collection of numbers

Map applies the inc function to each member of the passed collection and returns a new collection, what we expect is a collection containing [2 3 4 5 6 7].

Functions in Clojure

Now let's check how a function definition is essentially the same as the previous two forms:

```
(defn some-function [times parameter]
"Prints a string certain number of times"
  (dotimes [x times]
    (println parameter)))
```

The defn is the operation that we are asking for. It has several parameters, such as:

- some-function is the name of the function that we are defining
- [times parameter] is a collection of parameters
- "Prints a string certain number of times" is the docstring, it is actually an optional parameter
- (dotimes [x times] (println parameter)) is the body of the function that gets executed when you call some-function

The defn calls a function into existence. After this piece of code is executed, some-function exists in the current namespace and you can use it with the defined parameters.

The defn is actually written in Clojure and supports a few nice things. Let's now define a multi-arity function:

```
(defn hello
  ([] (hello "Clojure"))
  ([name] (str "Hello " name)))
```

Over here we are defining a function with two bodies, one of them has no arguments and the other one has one argument. It is actually pretty simple to understand what's happening.

Try changing the source in your project's core.clj file similar to the following example:

```
(ns getting-started.core
  (:gen-class))

(defn hello
  ([] (hello "Clojure"))
  ([name] (str "Hello " name)))

(defn -main
"I don't do a whole lot ... yet."
  [& args]
  (println "Hello, World!")
  (println (hello))
  (println (hello "Edu")))
```

Now run it, you'll get three different Hello outputs.

As you can see, Clojure has a very regular syntax and even if it's a little strange for newcomers, it is actually quite simple.

Here, we have used a few data types that we haven't properly introduced; in the next section we'll take a look at them.

Clojure's data types

Now is when everything you know about Java pays off; even the list forms that you saw earlier implement the java.util.List interface. Clojure was designed to be embeddable and to have a great integration with the host platform, so it's only natural that you can use everything you already know about Java types and objects.

There are two data types in Clojure: scalars and collections.

Scalars

In every language you need primitive types; you use them in everyday life as they represent numbers, strings, and Booleans. These primitive types are called scalars in the Clojure world.

Clojure has a couple of very interesting types like ratios and keywords. In the following table, you get to know the different types of scalars, how they compare to Java and a simple example of how to use each of them.

Clojure data type	Java data type	Sample	Description
String	String	"This is a string" "This is a multiline string"	A string of characters; in Clojure you can use multiline strings without a problem
Boolean	Boolean	true false	Literal Boolean values

Character	Character	`\c`
		`\u0045 ;;`
		`Unicode char`
		`45 E`
			Character values, they are `java.lang.Character` instances, you can define Unicode characters

Keywords	Doesn't exist in java	`:key`
		
		`:sample`
		
		`:some-keyword`
			They evaluate themselves and they are often used as keys. They are also functions that look for themselves in a map.

Number	Numbers are automatically handled as `BigDecimal`, `BigInteger` or lower precision depending on what's necessary	`42N ;;Big`
		`Integer`
		`42 ;;long`
		`0.1M`
		`;;BigDecimal`
			It is important to remember the trade-offs of Java numbers, if precision is important, you should always use big decimals and `bigintegers`.

Clojure data type	Java data type	Sample	Description
Ratio	Doesn't exist	22/7	Clojure provides great numerical precision; if necessary it can retain the ration and execute exact operation. The tradeoff when using ratios is speed.
Symbol	Doesn't exist	some-name	Symbols are identifiers in Clojure, very similar to a variable name in Java.
nil	null	nil	The null value
Regular expressions	`java.util.regex.Pattern`	`#"\d"`	Regular expressions, in Clojure you get free syntax to define regular expressions, but in the end it is a plain old Java reggae Pattern

Collection data types

In Clojure there are two types of collections: sequential and associative collections. Sequential are things you can iterate, such as lists. Associative collections are maps, sets, and things you can access by a certain index. Clojure's collections are fully compatible with Java and it can even implement the `java.util` interfaces, such as `java.util.List` and `java.util.Map`.

One of the main characteristics of collections in Clojure is that they are immutable; it has a lot of benefits that we'll see later.

Let's have a look at the characteristics of each collection data type available in Clojure and compare them with Java with the help of a sample (in Clojure) and its description.

Clojure data type	Java data type	Sample	Description
List	List	(1 2 3 4 5)	A simple list, notice the quote character before the list, if you don't specify it Clojure will try to evaluate the form as an instruction
Vector	Array	[1 2 3 4 5]	It is the main workhorse in Clojure, it is similar to an array because you can access elements in a random order
Set	HashSet	#{1 2 3 4}	A normal Java hash set
Map	HashMap	{:key 5 :key-2 "red"}	A Clojure map

Summary

As you can see, Clojure has a mature development environment that is always evolving. You can set up command-line tools and your IDE in a very similar fashion to the way you will do in a normal Java development.

We also learned a little about Clojure's regular syntax, its data types and how they relate to Java's own data types.

Overall, you should now be comfortable with:

- Lisp syntax
- Creating a Leiningen project from scratch
- Running and packaging your code
- Importing a Leiningen project into IntelliJ
- Using the REPL
- Knowing the relationship between Clojure types and Java types

In the next chapter, we will get an idea of how to organize our code and how that organization takes advantage of Java packages.

2
Namespaces, Packages, and Tests

We now have a working installation of Clojure and IntelliJ.

As a Java developer, you are used to working with classes as the minimal unit of organization. Clojure has a very different sense and gives you different tools to organize your code.

For starters, you should keep in mind that code and data are separate; you don't have a minimal unit with attributes and functions that work over those attributes. Your functions can work on any data structure that you wish, as long as you follow the rules of how the function works.

In this chapter, we will start writing some simple functions to illustrate how separation of functions and data works and we will have a look at the tools Clojure gives us to make the separation.

In this chapter, we will cover the following topic:

- How namespaces work compared to the classpath and Java packages
- Unit tests
- More Clojure examples and syntax

Namespaces in Clojure

Clojure namespaces might be familiar to you, as a Java developer, and for a very good reason, they have a very deep relationship with Java's packages and the classpath.

First of all, let's review what we already know from Java.

Packages in Clojure

The Java code is organized in packages, a package in Java is a namespace that allows you to group a set of similar classes and interfaces.

You can think of a package as something very similar to a folder in your computer.

The following are some common packages that you use a lot when programming in Java:

- `java.lang`: Everything that's native to Java, including basic types (integer, long, byte, boolean, character, string, number, short, float, void, and class), the basic threading primitives (runnable, thread), the basic primitives for exceptions (throwable, error, exception), the basic exceptions and errors (`NoSuchMethodError`, `OutOfMemoryError`, `StackOverflowError`, and so on) and runtime access classes like runtime and system.

- `java.io`: This package includes the primitives for input and output, such as console, file, readers, input streams, and writers.

- `java.util`: This is one of the most heavily used packages besides `java.lang`. This includes the classic data structures (map, set, list) along with the most common implementations of such data structures. This package also includes utilities like properties tools, scanner for reading from various input resources, `ServiceLoader` to load custom services from the `classloader`, UUID generator, timers, and so on.

- `java.util.logging`: The logging utilities, you normally use them to give you different levels of alert, from a debug to serious conditions.

- `java.text`: These are utilities to manage text, dates, and numbers in a language independent way.

- `javax.servlet`: This includes the primitives to create web apps and deployment in standard web containers.

Each one of these packages groups several related functionalities, the `java.lang` package is particularly important, since it has every Java core type, such as string, long, and integer. Everything inside the `java.lang` package is available automatically everywhere.

The `java.lang` package provides a bit more than just code organization, it also provides access security. If you remember about Java, there are three security access levels:

- private
- public
- protected

In the case of packages, we are concerned with the protected level of access. The classes in the same package allow every other class in the same package to access its protected attributes and methods.

There are also ways to analyze a package in runtime but they are involved and allow for very little to be done.

Packages are implemented at the top of Java's classpath and the classloader.

The classpath and the classloader

Java was designed to be modular and for that it needs some way to load your code easily. The answer to this was the classloader, the classloader allows you to read resources from every entry of the classpath; you can look at resources in the classpath as a hierarchical structure similar to the file system.

The classloader is just a list of entries; each entry can be a directory in the filesystem or a JAR file. At this point, you should also know that JAR files are just zip files.

The classloader will treat each entry as a directory (JAR files are just zipped directories) and it will look for files in each directory.

There are a lot of concepts here to remember, let's try to summarize them:

- JAR files are ZIP files; they might contain several classes, properties, files, and so on.
- The classpath is a list of entries; each entry is a JAR file or a system directory.
- The classloader looks for resources in each entry of the classpath, so you can think of classpath resources as a combination of all the directories in the classpath (repeated resources are not overwritten)

If you are not already familiar with how classloaders look for resources in classpath entries, this is the general process; let's imagine that you want to load a class: `test.Test`, what happens next?

1. You tell the JVM that you want to load `test.Test`.
2. The JVM knows to look for the `test/Test.class` file.
3. It starts looking for it in each entry of the classpath.
4. If the resource is a ZIP file, it "unzips" the directory.
5. It looks for the resource in the directory which represents the entry.

If you were to see the default classpath resources, you will probably see something, such as:

```
java:
    lang:
        String.class
        ....
    io:
        IOException.class
        ...
    util:
        List.class
```

It is important to note that each entry in the classpath doesn't just store class files, it can actually store any type of resource, It is a commonplace to store configuration files, such as `.properties` or `.xml`.

Nothing forbids you from storing anything else in the classpath resources, such as images, mp3 or even code! You can read and access anything from the classpath's resource like you can from the filesystem at runtime. The one thing that you can't do is modify the classpath's resource contents (at least not without some esoteric magic).

Back to Clojure namespaces

Now that we have had our little review of how packages and the classpaths work in Java, it's time to go back to Clojure. You should understand that Clojure attempts to make the hosting platform transparent; this means a couple of very important things:

- Anything that you can do with the classpath from Java, you can also do with Clojure (you can read configuration files, images, etc).
- Namespaces use the classpath just as Java does with packages, which makes them easy to understand. Nevertheless, don't underestimate them, Clojure namespace declarations can be more involved.

Let's get practical and play a little with namespaces.

Playing with namespaces

Lets create a new Playground, in order to create it use the following command:

```
lein new app ns-playground
```

You can open this project with IntelliJ, as we did in *Chapter 1, Getting Started with Clojure.*

Let's look in detail at what was created for us:

```
.
├── CHANGELOG.md
├── LICENSE
├── README.md
├── doc
│   └── intro.md
├── project.clj
├── resources
├── src
│   └── ns_playground
│       └── core.clj
└── test
    └── ns_playground
        └── core_test.clj

6 directories, 7 files
```

This project structure looks similar to Java projects, we have:

- resources: These are the non-source files that get added to the classpath
- src: Our source code
- test: Our testing code

The code inside `src` and `test` is already structured into namespaces: by having a quick look, we could say that the name of the namespace is `ns_playground`. Let's check the source code:

```clojure
(ns ns-playground.core
  (:gen-class))

(defn -main
"I don't do a whole lot ... yet."
  [& args]
  (println "Hello, World!"))
;; Code for src/ns_playground/core.clj
```

 `:gen-class` was added here in order to create a Java class and allow the Java interpreter to start a static main method. It is not needed if you don't intend to create a standalone program.

We can see that the `(ns ns-playground.core)` form has been used at the top, as you might have guessed, this is how we declare a namespace in Clojure.

If you are observant, you will notice something odd; the namespace has a dash instead of an underscore like the folder.

There are some reasons that lead to this:

- Clojure like most lisp variable names can have dashes in it (it is actually the preferred style to name the variables, as opposed to camel case in Java).
- Every namespace in Clojure is represented as a package containing several Java classes. The namespace is used as a name of the Java package and as you know, the dash is not acceptable in class or package names; so every filename and folder name must have low dashes.

 Due to the nature of Lisp, you can use dashes in variable names (they will get converted to underscores at compile time). In fact, this is the recommended way to name your variables. In Clojure, (and most Lisps) `some-variable-name` is a more idiomatic style than `someVariableName`.

Creating a new namespace

Let's create a new namespace; in Cursive Clojure it is easy to do so, just right-click on the `ns_playground` package and go to **New** | **Clojure Namespace**, it asks for a name and we can call it `hello`.

This creates a `hello.clj` file with the following contents:

```
(ns ns-playground.hello)
```

As you can see, namespace creation is quite easy; you can do it by hand with two simple steps:

1. Create a new file; it doesn't have to follow the package naming specification, but it helps to maintain your code order and it is a de facto practice.

2. Add your namespace declaration.

That's it! It is true, even though a namespace definition can become quite complex, as it is the place where you define the Java packages that you wish to import, namespaces or functions from those namespaces that you intend to use. But you will normally just use a subset of those capabilities.

 Keep in mind that a namespace in Clojure is normally represented by a single file.

For your initial namespaces, I will advice you to have two of those capabilities in mind:

`:import`	Allows you to import the Java classes from a package that you wish to use
`:require`	Allows you to bring in whatever Clojure namespace that you wish to use

The syntax of both `require` and the `import` is simple, let's look at a couple of examples before we actually use it.

Let's start with the `import` option:

```
(:import java.util.List)
```

You'll notice that this is similar to what you can do in Java, we are importing the `List` interface here.

The good thing with Clojure is that it allows you to do some more specific things. Let's check how to import two classes at once:

```
(:import [java.util ArrayList HashMap])
```

You can extend this to the number of classes you want to use.

The `require` option uses a similar syntax and then builds some more on it. Let's check requiring a single function from a namespace:

```
(:require [some.package :refer [a-function another-function]])
```

As you can see, it is familiar and the interesting part is when you start importing everything:

```
(:require [some.package :refer [:all]])
```

You can also use a custom name for everything inside your package:

```
(:require [some.package :as s])

;; And then use everything in the package like this:

(s/a-function 5)
```

Or you could even combine different keywords:

```
(:require [some.package :as s :refer [a-function]])
```

Let's try a bit of what we just learned, using the following code:

```
(ns ns-playground.hello
  (:import [java.util Date]))

(def addition +)

(defn current-date []
"Returns the current date"
  (new Date))

(defn <3 [love & loved-ones]
"Creates a sequence of all the {loved-ones} {loved} loves"
  (for [loved-one loved-ones]
    (str love " love " loved-one)))

(defn sum-something [something & nums]
"Adds something to all the remaining parameters"
  (apply addition something nums))

(def sum-one (partial sum-something 1))
```

You must have noticed the & operator in the arguments of the <3 and sum-something functions; this allows those functions to receive any number of arguments and we can call them, as shown: (sum-something 1 2 3 4 5 6 7 8) or (sum-something) They are called **variadic** functions. In Java you will call this feature **varargs**.

Everything looks great, but we haven't yet seen how to require and use these functions from some other package. Let's write a test to see how this will be done.

Working with namespaces on the REPL

A great way of playing with namespaces is by using the REPL and we'll also get the benefit of getting to know it better.

Since we are going to play with namespace, we need to know of a few functions that will help us move between namespaces and require other namespaces. The functions are listed as follows:

Function	Description	Sample usage
in-ns	Sets *ns* to the namespace named by the symbol, creating it if needed.	(in-ns 'ns-playground.core)
require	Loads libs, skipping any that are already loaded.	(require '[clojure.java.io :as io])
import	For each name in class-name-symbols, adds a mapping from name to the class named by package.name to the current namespace.	(import java.util.Date)
refer	refers to all public vars of ns, subject to filters.	(refer 'clojure.string :only '[capitalize trim])

Let's go into the REPL window of our IntelliJ. We can check what namespace we are in with the *ns* instruction. Let's try now:

```
*ns*
=> #<Namespace ns-playground.core>
```

Imagine that we need to execute a code and test the code from within the ns-playground.hello namespace, we can do that with the in-ns function:

```
(in-ns 'ns-playground.hello)
=> #<Namespace ns-playground.hello>
```

We want to know what str does, it seems to receive three strings:

```
(str "Hello""""world")
=>"Hello world"
```

Let's try the for form now:

```
(for [el ["element1""element2""element3"]] el)
=> ("element1""element2""element3")

(for [el ["element1""element2""element3"]]
  (str "Hello " el))
=> ("Hello element1""Hello element2""Hello element3")
```

The for macro takes a collection of items and returns a new lazy sequence applying the body of the for to each element.

Knowing this, understanding the <3 function is easy, let's try it:

```
(<3 "They""tea")
=> ("They love tea")

(clojure.repl/doc <3)
ns-playground.hello/<3
([& loved-ones])
  Creates a sequence of all the {loved-ones} {loved} loves
```

We've used the REPL to test some simple functions, but let's now try to test something else like reading a properties file from the classpath.

We can add a test.properties file to the resources folder with the following contents:

```
user=user
test=password
sample=5
```

Remember to restart the REPL, as the changes to the contents that some piece of the classpath points to are not visible to a running REPL.

Let's try reading our properties file as an input stream, we can use the `clojure.java.io` namespace to do it, and we can check it as shown:

```
(require '[clojure.java.io :as io])
(io/resource "test.properties")
=> #<URL file:/Users/iamedu/Clojure4Java/ns-playground/resources/test.
properties>
(io/input-stream (io/resource "test.properties"))
=> #<BufferedInputStream java.io.BufferedInputStream@2f584e71>
;; Let's now load it into a properties object
(import [java.util Properties])
=> java.util.Properties
(def props (Properties.)) ;; Don't worry about the weird syntax, we
will look it soon.
=> #'ns-playground.core/props
(.load props (io/input-stream (io/resource "test.properties")))
props
=> {"user""user", "sample""5", "test""password"}
```

We can now define our function for reading properties, we can input this into the REPL:

```
(defn read-properties [path]
  (let [resource (io/resource path)
        is (io/input-stream resource)
        props (Properties.)]
    (.load props is)
    (.close is)
    props))
=> #'ns-playground.core/read-properties
(read-properties "test.properties")
=> {"user""user", "sample""5", "test""password"}
```

> The `let` form lets us create local 'variables', instead of using the (`io/resource path`) directly in the code. We can create a reference once and use it through the code. It allows us to use simpler code and to have a single reference to an object.

In the end, we can redefine the `hello` namespace to include everything we've checked, such as this:

```clojure
(ns ns-playground.hello
  (:require [clojure.java.io :as io])
  (:import [java.util Date Properties]))

(def addition +)

(defn current-date []
"Returns the current date"
  (new Date))

(defn <3 [love & loved-ones]
"Creates a sequence of all the {loved-ones} {loved} loves"
  (for [loved-one loved-ones]
    (str love " love " loved-one)))

(defn sum-something [something & nums]
"Adds something to all the remaining parameters"
  (apply addition something nums))

(defn read-properties [path]
  (let [resource (io/resource path)
        is (io/input-stream resource)
        props (Properties.)]
    (.load props is)
  props))


(def sum-one (partial sum-something 1))
```

Remember to include the `Properties` class in the `import` and to define the `:require` keyword for `clojure.java.io`.

Testing in Clojure

Clojure already comes with a unit testing support built-in, as a matter of fact Leiningen has already created a test for us; let's take a look at it right now.

Open the `test/ns_playground/core_test.clj` file, you should be able to see this code:

```
(ns ns-playground.core-test
  (:require [clojure.test :refer :all]
            [ns-playground.core :refer :all]))
(deftest a-test
  (testing "FIXME, I fail."
(is (= 0 1))))
```

Again, as you can see, we are using `:require` to include functions from the `clojure.test` and the `ns-playground.core` packages.

 Remember, the `:refer` `:all` works similar to how char `import static clojure.test.*` will work in Java.

Testing from the command line

Let's first learn how to run these tests. From the command line, you can run:

`lein test`

You should get the following output:

```
lein test ns-playground.core-test

lein test :only ns-playground.core-test/a-test

FAIL in (a-test) (core_test.clj:7)
FIXME, I fail.
expected: (= 0 1)
  actual: (not (= 0 1))

Ran 1 tests containing 1 assertions.
1 failures, 0 errors.
Tests failed.
```

We see that there is one test failing, we will go back to this in a bit; for now, let's see how to test in IntelliJ.

Testing in IntelliJ

First of all, we need a new REPL configuration. You can do it as you learned in the previous chapter. You just need to follow the following steps:

1. Right click on the `project.clj` file and select **Create REPL for ns-playground,** as shown in the following screenshot:

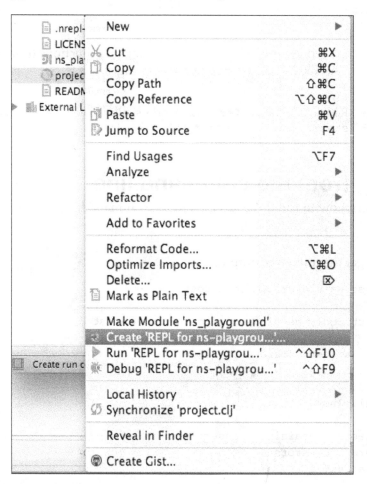

2. Then click on **OK** in the next dialog.

3. After that, you should run the REPL again by right clicking the `project.clj` file and selecting **Run REPL for ns-playground**.

4. After that you can run any tests, just open your test file and go to **Tools | Run Tests** in the current NS in REPL. You should see something similar to the following screenshot:

```
(ns ns-playground.core-test
  (:require [clojure.test :refer :all]
            [ns-playground.core :refer :all]))

(deftest a-test
  (testing "FIXME, I fail."
    (is (= 0 1))))
```

5. As you can see, it signals that your test is currently failing. Let's fix it and run our test again. Change the `(is (= 0 1))` line to `(is (= 1 1))`.

6. Now, let's try some real tests for our previously defined functions; don't worry if you can't understand all the code for now, you are not supposed to:

```
(ns ns-playground.hello-test
  (:import [java.util Date])
  (:require [clojure.test :refer :all]
            [ns-playground.hello :as hello :refer [<3]]
            [ns-playground.core :refer :all]))

(defn- lazy-contains? [col element]
  (not (empty? (filter #(= element %) col))))

(deftest a-test
  (testing "DONT FIXME, I don't fail."
    (is (= 42 42))))

(deftest current-date-is-date
  (testing "Test that the current date is a date"
    (is (instance? Date (hello/current-date)))))

(deftest check-loving-collection
  (testing "Check that I love clojure and you"
    (let [loving-seq (<3 "I""Clojure""you""doggies""chocolate")]
      (is (not (lazy-contains? loving-seq "I love Vogons")))
      (is (lazy-contains? loving-seq "I love Clojure"))
      (is (lazy-contains? loving-seq "I love doggies"))
      (is (lazy-contains? loving-seq "I love chocolate"))
      (is (lazy-contains? loving-seq "I love you")))))
```

We can't use the Clojure contents function here because it has a different function. It looks for keys in a map.

Run the tests and you'll see that everything passes correctly but there's a lot going on over here, let's go over it little by little:

```
(ns ns-playground.core-test
  (:import [java.util Date])
  (:require [clojure.test :refer :all]
            [ns-playground.hello :as hello :refer [<3]]
            [ns-playground.core :refer :all]))
```

This is the namespace declaration, let's list everything it does:

- It declares the `ns-playground.core-test` package.
- It imports the `java.util.Date` class.
- It makes everything in the `clojure.test` namespace available in the current namespace, if we were in Java we might have used `import static clojure.test.*` to get a similar effect. We can achieve this with the `:refer :all` keywords.
- It makes everything in the `ns-playground.hello` namespace available with the hello shortcut but we need to prefix every function or value defined in `ns-playground.hello` with hello and it also makes the `<3` function available without a prefix. To generate an alias and make everything available with the `hello` alias, we use the `:as` keyword and then pass a vector to `:refer` to include certain elements.
- It makes everything in the `ns-playground.core` namespace available in the current namespace. We achieve this with the `:refer :all` keywords.

```
(defn- lazy-contains? [col element]
  (not (empty? (filter #(= element %) col))))
```

This is the declaration of a function called `lazy-contains?`, it is a `boolean` function and it is customary in Clojure to call it a predicate.

 The name of the function including the question mark might be something that looks awkward to you. In Clojure and Lisp, you can use question marks in the names of functions and it is common to do it for functions that return Booleans.

It receives two parameters: `col` and `element`.

The actual body of the function looks a bit complicated but it is actually very simple. Whenever you encounter a function that looks similar to the one mentioned in the preceding section, try to read it from the inside out. The innermost part is, as follows:

```
#(= element %)
```

This is a shorter way of writing an anonymous function which has a single parameter. If we want to write another function that compares its argument against the element, without the syntactic sugar, we can do it in the following method:

```
(fn [el]
  (= element el))
```

This is an anonymous function or in other words it is a function that has no name, but it works as every other function; we will read more about anonymous functions when we get back to functional programming.

Our anonymous function is a parameter to the following form:

```
(filter #(= element %) col)
```

This new form filters the collection col and returns a new collection with only the elements that pass the test. Let's see an example where we have used the predefined Clojure function even?:

```
;; This returns only the even numbers in the collection
(filter even? [1 2 3 4])
;;=> (2 4)
```

Our filter function now returns every element in the collection that passes the `#(= element %)` test. So we get every element that is equal to the element passed to `lazy-contains?`.

We then ask if none of the elements equal to element in col with the following form:

```
(empty? (filter #(= element %) col))
```

But we want to know if there is some element equal to element, so at last we negate the previous form:

```
(not (empty? (filter #(= element %) col)))
```

Imagine that if you had to write this in Java (and I asked to add every element that matches the element to a list), you will have something similar to this:

```
List<T> filteredElements = new ArrayList<T>();
for(T el : col) {
    if(el == element) {
        filteredElements.add(el);
    }
}
return !filteredElements.isEmpty();
```

There is a big difference, it is more verbose and to understand it we need to "run" the algorithm in our heads. This is called imperative programming, Clojure allows us to do imperative programming as well as functional programming, which is a type of declarative programming. When you get used to it, you'll see that it's easier to reason about than loops.

 Interactive programming means, telling every step of how something should be done to a computer. Declarative programming just asks for a result and doesn't give details of how to achieve it.

The actual tests are simple to understand:

```
(deftest current-date-is-date
  (testing "Test that the current date is a date"
    (is (instance? Date (hello/current-date)))))
```

This test checks the current date returns an instance of `java.util.Date`, the is form works as the Java assert instruction:

```
(deftest check-loving-collection
  (testing "Check that I love clojure and you"
    (let [loving-seq (<3 "I""Clojure""you""doggies""chocolate")]
      (is (not (lazy-contains? loving-seq "I love Vogons")))
      (is (lazy-contains? loving-seq "I love Clojure"))
      (is (lazy-contains? loving-seq "I love doggies"))
      (is (lazy-contains? loving-seq "I love chocolate"))
      (is (lazy-contains? loving-seq "I love you")))))
```

This test checks the <3 function, it checks that the returned collection contains I love Clojure, I love doggies, I love chocolate and I love you and it should not contain I love Vogons.

This test is simple to understand. What might be not so simple to understand is the <3 function, we'll look into it with the REPL.

Summary

In this chapter, we got to know some utilities that we can use for better management of our code and we have some more examples of everyday Clojure code. In particular:

- Working of namespace in Clojure and their relation to Java packages
- Writing out-of-the-box unit tests and executing them with Leiningen and Cursive Clojure
- Delving into the Clojure Interactive development workflow and a bit of the Clojure mindset
- Writing very simple functions and testing them

In the next chapter, we will learn about Java interop, so we can start using the familiar classes and libraries we already know in our Clojure code.

We will also learn how to use Clojure from Java, so you can start using it in your everyday Java projects.

Interacting with Java

3

We know a bit about how to organize our code and how that relates to packages in Java. Now, you surely need to use your old Java code and all the libraries you already know; Clojure encourages a new way to think about programming and it also allows you to use all the dependencies and code that you've already generated.

Clojure is a **Java Virtual Machine (JVM)** language and as such it is compatible with most Java dependencies and libraries out there; you should be able to use all the tools out there. You should also be able to use your Clojure programs with Java-only programs, this requires a bit of custom coding but in the end you can use Clojure in the right places of your project.

To be able to do this, we'll have to learn:

- Using Maven dependencies
- Using plain old Java classes from your Clojure code base
- A bit more about the Clojure language, in particular the `let` statements and destructuring
- Creating a Java interface for your Clojure code
- Using the Java interface from other Java projects

Using Maven dependencies

Let's say that we want to write an image manipulation program; it is a very simple program that should be able to create thumbnails. Most of our codebase is in Clojure, so we want to write this in Clojure too.

There are a bunch of Java libraries meant to manipulate images, we decide to use imgscalr, which is very simple to use and it looks like it is available in Maven Central (http://search.maven.org/).

Let's create a new Leiningen project, as shown:

```
lein new thumbnails
```

Now, we need to edit the project.clj file in the thumbnails project:

```
(defproject thumbnails "0.1.0-SNAPSHOT"
  :description "FIXME: write description"
  :url "http://example.com/FIXME"
  :license {:name "Eclipse Public License"
            :url "http://www.eclipse.org/legal/epl-v10.html"}
  :dependencies [[org.clojure/clojure "1.6.0"]])
```

You can add the imgscalr dependency similar to the following code:

```
(defproject thumbnails "0.1.0-SNAPSHOT"
  :description "FIXME: write description"
  :url "http://example.com/FIXME"
  :license {:name "Eclipse Public License"
            :url "http://www.eclipse.org/legal/epl-v10.html"}
  :dependencies [[org.clojure/clojure "1.6.0"]
                 [org.imgscalr/imgscalr-lib "4.2"]])
```

As you can see, you just need to add a dependency to the :dependencies vector, the dependencies are automatically resolved from:

- Maven Local
- Maven Central
- Clojars

 The Maven Local points to your local maven repository that is in the ~/.m2 folder. If you wish, you can change it with Leiningen's :local-repo key.

You can add your own repositories, let's say you need to add **jcenter** (Bintray's Java repository) you can do so, as shown:

```
(defproject thumbnails "0.1.0-SNAPSHOT"
  :description "FIXME: write description"
  :url "http://example.com/FIXME"
```

```
:license {:name "Eclipse Public License"
          :url "http://www.eclipse.org/legal/epl-v10.html"}
:dependencies [[org.clojure/clojure "1.6.0"]
               [org.imgscalr/imgscalr-lib "4.2"]]
:repositories [["jcenter" "http://jcenter.bintray.com/"]])
```

 Leiningen supports a wide array of options to configure your project, for more information you can check the sample at Leiningen's official repository: https://github.com/technomancy/leiningen/blob/master/sample.project.clj.

In order to download the dependencies, you have to execute the following code:

lein deps

 You don't need to execute lein deps every time you want to download dependencies, you can do it to force a download but Leiningen will automatically download them when it needs to.

You can check the current dependencies by running:

lein deps :tree

You will get something similar to this:

```
[clojure-complete "0.2.3" :scope "test" :exclusions [[org.clojure/
clojure]]]
[org.clojure/clojure "1.6.0"]
[org.clojure/tools.nrepl "0.2.6" :scope "test" :exclusions [[org.
clojure/clojure]]]
[org.imgscalr/imgscalr-lib "4.2"]
```

This lists your current dependency tree.

Clojure interop syntax

Clojure was designed to be a Hosted Language, which means that it can run in different environments or runtimes. One important philosophy aspect is that Clojure does not attempt to get in the way of your original host; this allows you to use your knowledge of the underlying platform to your advantage.

In this case, we are using the Java platform. Let's look at the basic interrupt syntax that we need to know.

Creating an object

There are two ways to create an object in Clojure; for example, let's have a look at how to create an instance of `java.util.ArrayList`.

```
(def a (new java.util.ArrayList 20))
```

Here, we are using the `new` special form, as you can see it receives a symbol (the name of the class `java.util.ArrayList`) and in this case it is an integer.

The symbol `java.util.ArrayList` represents the `classname` and any Java class name will do here.

Next, you can actually pass any number of parameters (including 0 parameters). The next parameters are the parameters of the constructor.

Lets have a look at the other special syntax that is available to create objects:

```
(def a (ArrayList.))
```

The difference here is that we have a trailing dot; we prefer to see this syntax since it is shorter.

Calling an instance method

Once we have created our object we can call instance methods. This is done similar to how we call Clojure functions, using the special dot form.

If we want to add an element to our newly created list, we will have to do it, as shown:

```
(. add a 5)
```

This syntax might look a little strange; here is how this syntax is formed:

```
(. instance method-name args*)
```

Similar to the two different options that we had when creating an object, we have another way to do this:

```
(.method-name instance args*)
```

You might think that this is more familiar, since the method name starting with a dot resembles how we write the Java method calls.

Calling a static method or function

Being able to call methods and create objects gives us a great deal of power, with this simple construct we have gained a lot of power; we can now use most of the Java standard libraries and also the custom ones.

However, we still need a few more things; one of the most important ones is calling static methods. The static methods have a feel similar to Clojure functions, there is no `this` instance, you can simply call them as normal Clojure functions.

For instance, if we want an `emptyMap` from the `Collections` class, we can do it as shown:

```
(java.util.Collections/emptyMap)
```

You can think of static methods as functions and the class as a namespace. It is not exactly right but the mental model will help you understand it easily.

Accessing inner classes

Another common doubt when using Java – Clojure interop is how to access inner classes.

Imagine you want to represent a single entry from a map with the `java.util.AbstractMap.SimpleEntry` class.

You might think that we have to do something similar to this:

```
(java.util.AbstractMap.SimpleEntry. "key" "value")
```

That's what you will normally do when writing Java, but in Clojure you might need to do something such as this:

```
(java.util.AbstractMap$SimpleEntry. "key" "value")
```

What we are seeing here is actually an exposed implementation detail; if you look at the classes in the JAR files or in your classpath, you will see the precise file name `AbstractMap$SimpleEntry`, as shown in the following screenshot:

```
# iamedu at Eduardos-MacBook-Pro.local in /Library/Java/JavaVirtualMachines/jdk1.8.0_66.jdk/Contents/Home [5:53:37]
$ jar -tf ./jre/lib/rt.jar | grep AbstractMap
java/beans/MetaData$java_util_AbstractMap_PersistenceDelegate.class
java/util/AbstractMap$1$1.class
java/util/AbstractMap$1.class
java/util/AbstractMap$2$1.class
java/util/AbstractMap$2.class
java/util/AbstractMap$SimpleEntry.class
java/util/AbstractMap$SimpleImmutableEntry.class
java/util/AbstractMap.class
```

This is what you need to keep in mind, always prefix the inner classes with the parent (or more correctly containing) class (in this case `java.util.AbstractMap`) and the dollar sign.

Writing a simple image namespace

Let's now write some Clojure code and create a file in `src/thumbnails/image.clj`.

Let's try to do this the Clojure way. First of all, write the namespace declaration and evaluate it:

```
(ns thumbnails.image
  (:require [clojure.java.io :as io])
  (:import [javax.imageio ImageIO]
           [java.awt.image BufferedImageOp]
           [org.imgscalr Scalr Scalr$Mode]))
```

Now open up a REPL and write the following code:

```
(def image-stream (io/input-stream "http://imgs.xkcd.com/comics/
angular_momentum.jpg"))
(def image (ImageIO/read image-stream))
image
(.getWidth image)
```

We now have an image instance and you can call all of the Java methods in the REPL. This is one of Clojure's core concepts, you can play with the REPL and check your code before really writing it and you can do it in an interactive way, as shown:

```
user=> (def image-stream (io/input-stream "http://imgs.xkcd.com/comics/angular_momentum.jpg"))
#'user/image-stream
user=> (def image (ImageIO/read image-stream))
#'user/image
user=> image
#object[java.awt.image.BufferedImage 0x69a568f0 "BufferedImage@69a568f0: type = 10 ColorModel: #pixelBits = 8 numComponents = 1 color space
 = java.awt.color.ICC_ColorSpace@6e4f49da transparency = 1 has alpha = false isAlphaPre = false ByteInterleavedRaster: width = 600 height =
 386 #numDataElements 1 dataOff[0] = 0"]
user=> (.getHeight image)
386
user=>
```

In the end, we want to stick with the following contents:

```clojure
(ns thumbnails.image
  (:require [clojure.java.io :as io])
  (:import [javax.imageio ImageIO]
           [java.awt.image BufferedImageOp]
           [org.imgscalr Scalr Scalr$Mode]))


(defn load-image [image-stream]
  (ImageIO/read image-stream))

(defn save-image [image path]
  (ImageIO/write image "PNG" (io/output-stream path)))

(defn image-size [image]
  [(.getWidth image) (.getHeight image)])

(defn generate-thumbnail [image size]
  (Scalr/resize image Scalr$Mode/FIT_TO_WIDTH size (into-array
BufferedImageOp [])))

(defn get-image-width [image-path]
  (let [image (load-image image-path)
        [w _] (image-size image)]
    w))
```

> You can see that in this code we use the inner class syntax, with `Scalr$Mode`. Mode is not actually a class but an enum, you can use the same syntax for all other inner types.

The code is pretty simple, it is very similar to what you've already seen; we'll go through the differences either way.

You can import the following classes:

- `javax.imageio.ImageIO`
- `java.awt.image.BufferedImageOp`
- `org.imgscalr.Scalr`
- `org.imgscalr.Scalr.Mode`

You have to be careful with the `Mode` class, since it is an inner class (it is inside another class) Clojure uses the special name `Scalr$Mode`.

 When importing inner classes, you have to be careful with the naming process, in Java you will use the name: `org.imgscalr.Scalr.Mode`; in Clojure you use the name: `org.imgscalr.Scalr$Mode`. The load-image, save-image, and `image-size` functions are self explanatory and the `generate-thumbnail` function is pretty simple as well; however, it has a special detail, it calls the following as the last argument:

```
(into-array BufferedImageOp [])
```

If you look at the ImageScalr javadoc, (`http://javadox.com/org.imgscalr/imgscalr-lib/4.2/org/imgscalr/Scalr.Mode.html`) you can see that the resize method has several overloaded implementations; most of them have a `varargs` argument as their last argument. In Clojure, you have to declare these `varargs` arguments as an array.

Writing the tests

Now that you have written your image processing code, it is a good time to write the tests.

Let's just check if we can generate a thumbnail. Create a new `thumbnails.thumbnail-test` namespace, in the tests.

Remember, if you create the file, it must be named `test/thumbnails/thumbnail_test.clj`.

Add the following contents to it:

```
(ns thumbnails.thumbnail-test
  (:require [clojure.test :refer :all]
            [clojure.java.io :as io]
            [thumbnails.image :refer :all]))

(deftest test-image-width
  (testing "We should be able to get the image with"
    (let [image-stream (io/input-stream "http://imgs.xkcd.com/comics/
angular_momentum.jpg")
          image (load-image image-stream)]
      (save-image image "xkcd-width.png")
      (is (= 600 (get-image-width (io/input-stream "xkcd-width.
png")))))))

(deftest test-load-image
  (testing "We should be able to generate thumbnails"
    (let [image-stream (io/input-stream "http://imgs.xkcd.com/comics/
angular_momentum.jpg")
          image (load-image image-stream)
          thumbnail-image (generate-thumbnail image 50)]
      (save-image thumbnail-image "xkcd.png")
      (is (= 50 (get-image-width (io/input-stream "xkcd.png")))))))
```

Here we are using some unknown features, such as the let form and destructuring. We will see this in more detail in the next section.

The let statement

Clojure gives us a let statement to name things; it allows us to do something very similar to variable declaration in other languages.

Keep in mind that we are not actually creating a variable in the same sense, as in Java. In Java, whenever we declare a variable. We state that we want to reserve a certain amount of memory to store something in the later stages; it can be a value for primitives or a memory location for objects. What we do here is simply name a value. This is a local scope that is useful to write cleaner and easier to understand code. Lets have a look at how it works:

```
(let [x 42] x)
```

This is the simplest `let` statement that we could write and it is exactly the same as just writing 42. However, we can write something a little more complex, such as this:

```
(let [x 42
      y (* x x)]
  (println "x is " x " and y " y))
```

It looks self explanatory; to value 42 and y, we are assigning the value of multiplying 42 by 42. In the end, we print x is 42 and y 1764. It is important to note two things here:

- We can use a previously defined value in the `let` statement; for example, we use x when defining y.

- The `let` statement creates a scope, we can't use x or y outside of our `let` statement.

The `let` statement can even be nested, we could do something similar to the following example:

```
(let [x 42]
  (let [y (* x x)]
    (println "x is " x " and y " y)))
```

It is a bit more complicated, since we are opening an unneeded set of parentheses and also writing more code; however, it allows us to see how lexical scope works.

Lets have a look at another interesting example:

```
(let [x 42]
  (let [y (* x x)]
    (let [x 41]
      (println "x is " x " and y " y))))
```

In here, we are masking the value of x with 41 and again these are not variables. We are not changing a memory region, we are merely creating a new scope with a new X value.

Going back to our test, the `let` statement begins with the following code:

```
image (load-image image-path)
```

It is pretty clear to understand, but the next line might prove a bit more difficult:

```
[w _] (image-size image)
```

It looks pretty strange; we are assigning the value of (image-size image) to [w _]
but [w _] is not a symbol name!

What is happening here is that we are using a mechanism called destructuring to
take the result of (image-size image) apart and just use the piece of information
that we are interested in, which in this case is the width of the image.

Destructuring is one of the key features of Clojure, it can be used almost everywhere
where symbol binding happens, such as:

- Let expressions
- Function parameter lists

Destructuring helps write more concise code but it might strike you as strange when
you are not used to it. Let's talk about it in depth in the next section.

Destructuring in Clojure

Destructuring is a feature in Clojure that is not common in other lisps; the idea is
to allow you to write more concise code in scenarios where code doesn't really add
value (for example, getting the first element from a list or the second parameter from
a function) and concentrating only on what is important to you.

In order to understand this better, let's see an example of why destructuring can
help you:

```
(let [v [1 2 3]] [(first v) (nth v 2)]) ;; [1 3]
```

What's wrong with the previous code? Nothing really, but you need to start thinking
about what is v, what the first value of v is, what the nth function does, and at what
index v starts.

Instead we can do this:

```
(let [[f s t] [1 2 3]] [f t]) ;; [1 3]
```

Once you are used to destructuring, you will see that you don't need to think about
how to get the elements you need. In this case, we directly access the first, second,
and third elements from our vector and use the first and third out of the three
elements. With good naming it can become even easier.

Lets now take a deep dive into what destructuring is.

There are two types of destructuring:

- **Sequential destructuring**: It allows us to take sequential data structures apart and bind the values that you are interested in directly to symbols

- **Associative destructuring**: It allows us to take maps apart and bind only the key reference values that you are interested in directly to symbols

Sequential destructuring

Sequential destructuring should be easy to understand with some examples; lets have a look:

```
(let [[f s] [1 2]] f) ;; 1
(let [[f s t] [1 2 3]] [f t]) ;; [1 3]
(let [[f] [1 2]] f);; 1
(let [[f s t] [1 2]] t);; nil
(let [[f & t [1 2]] t);; (2)
(let [[f & t [1 2 3]] t);; (2 3)
(let [[f & t [1 2 3]] t);; (2 3)
(let [[f & [_ t]] [1 2 3]] [f t])
```

In these examples, as convention, we use f for first, s for second, t for third, and a for all the others.

The same destructuring idea and syntax can be used with function parameters, as shown in the next example:

```
(defn func [[f _ t]]
  (+ f t))
(func [1 2 3]) ;; 4
```

 Here we use the symbol _, there is a convention in Clojure to use the _ symbol whenever you are not interested in some value and you don't need to use it in the future. In the previous example, we aren't interested in the second parameter of the func function.

As you can see, it lets us write a much more concise code and focus only on what's important, which is the algorithm or business.

Associative destructuring

We've already seen sequential destructuring that allows getting certain elements of a sequence by index. In Clojure, there is also associative destructuring, which allows you to take just the keys of the map in which you are interested.

Again, an example is worth more than a thousand words:

```
(let [{a-value a} {: a-value  5}] a-value) ;; 5
(let [{a-value :a c-value :c} {:a 5 :b 6 :c 7}] c-value) ;; 7
(let [{:keys [a c]} {:a 5 :b 6 :c 7}] c) ;; 7
(let [{:syms [a c]} {'a 5 :b 6 'c 7}] c) ;; 7
(let [{:strs [a c]} {:a 5 :b 6 :c 7 "a" 9}] [a c]) ;; [9 nil]
(let [{:strs [a c] :or {c 42}} {:a 5 :b 6 :c 7 "a" 9}] [a c]) ;; [9 42]
```

> Thinking of symbols as keys to a map can feel strange, nonetheless it is important to remember this feature; it could come in handy at some point.

As you can see, it's pretty simple too, but we have a few more options:

- We can reference some keys and assigning them a name, as shown in the first and second example
- We can reference keyword keys, as in the third example
- We can reference string keys, as in the fourth example
- We can define default values with the :or keyword!

Destructuring is one of the most used features of Clojure and it allows you to write very concise code.

Going back to our test code, it should now be pretty easy to understand the get-image-width function:

```
(defn get-image-width [image-path]
  (let [image (load-image image-path)
        [w _] (image-size image)]
    w))
```

As you can see, it sets the image value as the loaded image and then it calculates the width, gets the width only and returns that value.

We can now understand the `test-load-image` test:

```
(deftest test-load-image
  (testing "We should be able to generate thumbnails"
    (let [image-stream    (io/input-stream "http://imgs.xkcd.com/
comics/angular_momentum.jpg")
          image           (load-image image-stream)
          thumbnail-image (generate-thumbnail image 50)]
      (save-image thumbnail-image "xkcd.png")
      (is (= 50 (get-image-width (io/input-stream "xkcd.png")))))))))
```

It just initializes an `image-stream` value, it then loads an image from that stream and generates a thumbnail. It finally loads the generated thumbnail and checks that the image width is 50px.

Now that we've written our tests and we are sure that everything works, we can use our little library from the Clojure projects, but what happens if we want to use it from a pure Java (or groovy, or scala) project?

Exposing your code to Java

If you want to be able to use Clojure code from other JVM languages, in Clojure, there are a couple of ways in which you can do it:

- You can generate new Java classes and use them as you normally would; it can implement some interface or extend from some other class

- You can generate a proxy on the fly, this way you can implement a contract (in the form of a class or an interface) that some framework requires with little code and effort

- You can use the `clojure.java.api` package to call Clojure functions directly from Java

 You can find more information on how this works at the following location: `http://www.falkoriemenschneider.de/a__2014-03-22__Add-Awesomeness-to-your-Legacy-Java.html`.

Let's have a look at how we can define a Java class.

Create a new namespace called `thumbnails.image-java` and write the following code:

```
(ns thumbnails.image-java
  (:require [thumbnails.image :as img])
  (:gen-class
    :methods [[loadImage [java.io.InputStream] java.awt.image.
BufferedImage]
              [saveImage [java.awt.image.BufferedImage String] void]
              [generateThumbnail [java.awt.image.BufferedImage int]
java.awt.image.BufferedImage]]
    :main false
    :name thumbnails.ImageProcessor))

(defn -loadImage [this image-stream]
  (img/load-image image-stream))

(defn -saveImage [this image path]
  (img/save-image image path))

(defn -generateThumbnail [this image size]
  (img/generate-thumbnail image size))
```

This code is very similar to the Clojure code that we have already seen, except for the `gen-class` directive and the function names starting with a dash.

Let's review the `gem-class` in better detail:

```
(:gen-class
    :methods [[loadImage [java.io.InputStream] java.awt.image.
BufferedImage]
              [saveImage [java.awt.image.BufferedImage String] void]
              [generateThumbnail [java.awt.image.BufferedImage int]
java.awt.image.BufferedImage]]
    :main false
    :name thumbnails.ImageProcessor)
```

When the Clojure compiler sees this, it generates the byte code of a class but it needs a little help from the keywords to know how to generate the class.

- The name key defines the name of the class, it is a symbol
- The main key defines whether this class should have a main method or not
- The method key defines all the methods and their signatures, it is a vector with three parts: [methodName [parameterTypes] returnType]

The methods are then implemented as functions starting with the (-) character, the prefix can be changed with the prefix key.

You also need to tell Clojure to compile this class in advance, in Leiningen it can be achieved with :aot, go to your project.clj file and add an :aot key with the namespace or namespaces to be compiled in a vector; if you want everything to be compiled in advance, you could use the special :all value.

In the end, you should have something similar to this:

```
1  (defproject thumbnails "0.1.0-SNAPSHOT"
2    :description "FIXME: write description"
3    :url "http://example.com/FIXME"
4    :license {:name "Eclipse Public License"
5              :url "http://www.eclipse.org/legal/epl-v10.html"}
6    :dependencies [[org.clojure/clojure "1.6.0"]
7                   [org.imgscalr/imgscalr-lib "4.2"]]
8    :aot [thumbnails.image-java]
9    :repositories [["jcenter" "http://jcenter.bintray.com/"]])
```

 If you want all of your code to be compiled in advance, you can use :aot :all in your project.clj.

Now, we can install our library to our Maven local repository. Go to the command line and run:

```
$ lein install
```

You'll get an output similar to the following screenshot:

```
# iamedu at Eduardos-MacBook-Pro.local in ~/Development/clj/source/chapter03/initial/thumbnails [6:25:18]
$ lein install
Created /Users/iamedu/Development/clj/source/chapter03/initial/thumbnails/target/thumbnails-0.1.0-SNAPSHOT.jar
Wrote /Users/iamedu/Development/clj/source/chapter03/initial/thumbnails/pom.xml
Installed jar and pom into local repo.
```

Now, you are good to go; you should have a thumbnails:thumbnails:0.1.0-SNAPSHOT dependency in your Maven local repository.

Testing from Groovy

In order to see how this works with several JVM languages, we will use Groovy and Gradle to test. We can use Java and Maven just as easily. Remember that you can get the source from the code bundle so that you don't need to know everything that's happening here.

There are two files here; in the `build.gradle` file, we specify that we want to use our local Maven repository and we specify our dependency, as:

```
apply plugin: 'java'
apply plugin: 'groovy'

repositories {
  jcenter()
  mavenLocal()
}

dependencies {
  compile "thumbnails:thumbnails:0.1.0-SNAPSHOT"
  testCompile "org.spockframework:spock-core:0.7-groovy-2.0"
}
```

Then we can write our test, as the following code:

```
package imaging.java

import thumbnails.ImageProcessor
import spock.lang.*

class ImageSpec extends Specification {
  def "Test we can use imaging tools"() {
    setup:
      def processor = new ImageProcessor()
      def imageStream = getClass().getResourceAsStream("/test.png")

    when:
      def image = processor.loadImage(imageStream)
      def thumbnail = processor.generateThumbnail(image, 100)

    then:
      thumbnail.getWidth() == 100
  }
}
```

You can then run the tests:

```
gradle test
```

As you can see, it is very easy to run your code from Java, Groovy, or even Scala. There are other ways to use Clojure with Java, particularly, if you want to implement an interface or generate a class dynamically.

Proxy and reify

There are situations when you are interacting with Java libraries, where you must send an instance of a specific Java class to some method; writing a class isn't the best option, you should rather create an instance that conforms to a contract expected by some framework on the fly. We have two options to do this:

- **Proxy**: It allows you to implement a Java interface or extend from some super class. In reality, it creates a new object that calls your Clojure functions when needed

- **Reify**: Reify allows you to implement interfaces and Clojure protocols (we will see them later). It is not capable of extending classes. It is a better performant than the proxy and should be used whenever possible.

Let's look at a minimal example:

```
(import '(javax.swing JFrame JLabel JTextField JButton)
        '(java.awt.event ActionListener)
        '(java.awt GridLayout))
(defn sample []
  (let [frame (JFrame. "Simple Java Integration")
        sample-button (JButton. "Hello")]
    (.addActionListener
     sample-button
     (reify ActionListener
             (actionPerformed
               [_ evt]
               (println "Hello world"))))
    (doto frame
      (.add sample-button)
      (.setSize 100 40)
      (.setVisible true))))
(sample)
```

[doto is a macro that allows us to call several methods on an instance; you can think of it as a way to call all of the methods separately. It works great with Java Beans!]

Open up an REPL and write the code; it should show a window with a button that prints Hello world (in the terminal) when clicked:

```
user=> (sample)
#<JFrame javax.swing.JFrame[frame        yout=java.awt.BorderLayout,titl
e=Simple Java Integration,resizab            tCloseOperation=HIDE_ON_CLOSE,r
ootPane=javax.swing.JRootPane[,0,           =javax.swing.JRootPane$RootLayo
ut,alignmentX=0.0,alignmentY=0.0,            777673,maximumSize=,minimumSize
=,preferredSize=],rootPaneCheckingEnabled=true]>
user=> Hello world
Hello world
Hello world
Hello world
[]
```

If you are familiar with swing, then you know that the addActionListener of JButton needs a callback which is an instance of ActionListener and we are creating said instance with the reify function.

In Java code, you might normally do something similar to the following code:

```
button.addActionListener(new ActionListener() {
   public void actionPerformed(ActionEvent e) {
     System.out.println("Hello world")'
   }
})
```

We call this an anonymous class and it is essentially the same as a closure in functional languages. In the previous example, the code was replaced by a reify:

```
(reify ActionListener
         (actionPerformed
          [_ evt]
          (println "Hello world")))
```

The reify statement receives the interface that you are implementing and all the methods that you are implementing as you list. In this case, we just implement actionPerformed to receive the action event.

This is the structure:

```
(reify InterfaceOrProtocol
  (method [self parameter-list]
    method-body)
  (method2 [self parameter-list]
    method-body))
```

This creates an instance of `ActionListener`, you can do the same with servlets, threads, collections, lists, or any other Java interface defined by anyone.

One particular thing that you need to remember here is that you need to always add `self` as the first parameter to your method implementations; it takes the place of the `this` keyword that works in Java.

Summary

In this chapter, you have gained a lot of power from Clojure with a few new primitives.

As you can see, there are plenty of ways to interact with your current codebase; specifically, you can now:

- Use Java code from Clojure
- Use Clojure code from Java
- Reuse Java frameworks by creating objects that adhere to their contracts

With all of our new tools in mind, we are ready to tackle more concepts and a little bit more complexity with collections and data structures.

4
Collections and Functional Programming

We are now comfortable with using Java code from our Clojure programs, and we also know how to expose our Clojure programs with a Java API. However, we need to take a deeper look at Clojure and its true nature, which is functional programming.

In this chapter, we will cover the following topics:

- Basics of functional programming
- Persistent collections
- Sequential and associative collections
- The sequence abstraction
- Collection types
- Applying functional programming to collections

Basics of functional programming

This is a topic that you can read about in lots of different places, and it seems that everyone has their own opinion of what functional programming is. There is however, some common ground that you will find in almost every definition, which relates to the benefits you gain from functional programming, such as:

- Easier code reuse
- Functions are easier to test
- Functions are easier to reason about

In order to get these benefits, you need to take into account the following things:

- You should think of functions as first class citizens
- Functions should minimize side effects (they shouldn't change any state)
- Functions should only depend on their parameters (this is called referential transparency)

Lets take a look at two examples of functions (or methods) in Java to illustrate how, even in Java, you can get benefits from writing functions without side effects and context dependency.

```java
public void payRent(BigDecimal amount) {
  User user = getCurrentUser();
  if(user.payAmount != amount) {
    System.out.println("Cannot pay");
  } else {
    user.money -= amount;
  }
}
```

Imagine you had to test the preceding function; you might have a number of problems:

1. You need to know how to get the current user; you might need to mock a database, or session storage. Or in the worst case scenario, you might need a real session storage service.
2. How can you know if something was paid for or not?

Now, look at this other example:

```java
public boolean payRent(User user, BigDecimal amount, ValidateStrategy
strategy) {
  if(strategy.validatePayment(user, amount)) {
    user.money -= amount;
    return true;
  } else {
    return false;
  }
}
```

The preceding code is easier to test; you can create a user instance any way you want and with the `ValidateStrategy` class (or interface) you could do whatever you need.

In the end, instead of a side-effect you get a return value stating if the action was possible or not. This way you don't need to mock and you can reuse it in different contexts.

Now that we have seen some common ground for functional programming, let's take a look at Clojure's value proposition for functional programming:

- Functions are first class citizens or values. The same as with integers or strings, you can create them in runtime, pass them around, and receive them in other functions.

- The same way that functions are values, the data structures are also values; they can't be modified in the sense that they can be modified in Java but they are a fixed value, just as an integer is a fixed value.

- Immutable data structures are very important, they allow for safe and simple multithreaded code.

- Laziness (of data structures) allows deferring evaluation until needed, to execute just what you must.

Persistent collections

One of the most important features in Clojure is that collections are persistent. That does not mean that they are persistent to disk, it means that you can have several historical versions of a collection with the guarantee that updating or looking for something in any of those versions is going to have the same effort (complexity). You get all this with very little extra memory.

How? It is actually pretty simple. Clojure shares a common structure between several different data structures. If you add a single element to a data structure, Clojure shares the common part between the two structures and keeps track of the differences.

Let's see what we mean with an example:

```
(def sample-coll [:one :two :three])
(def second-sample-coll (conj sample-coll :four))
(def third-sample-coll (replace {:one 1} sample-coll))

sample-coll ;; [:one :two :three]
second-sample-coll ;; [:one :two :three :four]
third-sample-coll ;; [1 :two :three :four]
```

As you can see, when you `conj` a new item into a collection, or even when you replace some elements from it, you aren't changing the original collection, you are just generating a new version of it.

> In Clojure, you can use `conj` (conjoin) as a verb. It means adding new elements into a collection in an efficient manner.

This new version doesn't modify the previous collections you had in any way.

This is a big difference from how common imperative languages work and at the first glance it might seem like a bad idea, but Clojure uses efficient algorithms that give us a couple of advantages, specifically:

- Different versions of the same collection share common parts, allowing us to use little memory
- When some part of the collection is not visible it gets garbage collected

What you get out of this is similar memory usage to what you would have with a mutable collection. Remember that there is a cost in space and time but it is negligible for most use cases.

Why would you want to have an immutable data collection? The main advantage is that it is simple to reason about them; passing them around to functions does not change them and when you are writing concurrent code, there is no chance that some other thread has modified your collection and you don't need to worry about explicitly handling locks.

Types of collections in Clojure

There are three types of collections in Clojure: counted, sequential, and associative. They are not mutually exclusive, meaning one collection might be any.

Let's look at each type:

- **Counted collection**: A counted collection is a collection which knows its size in constant time. It doesn't need to traverse its elements to get a count.
- **Sequential collection**: A sequential collection can be traversed sequentially; it's the most common approach that you would use for a list. The easiest way to think about this is similar to Java's list, which you can traverse with a for-loop or an iterator. In Clojure vectors, lists and lazy sequences are sequential collections.

- **Associative collections**: Associative collections can be accessed by keys; maps are the natural choice here. We said that one collection can be of any type; Clojure's vectors can also be used as associative collections, and each element index can be used as a key. You can think of it as a map where the keys are 0, 1, 2, 3, and so on.

Clojure has some functions that tell us if a given collection is of each type, sequential or associative. As you can guess, vectors return true for both. The following are those functions:

Function name	List	Vector	Map	Lazy sequence	Set
counted?	true	true	true	false	true
sequential?	true	true	false	true	false
associative?	false	true	true	false	false

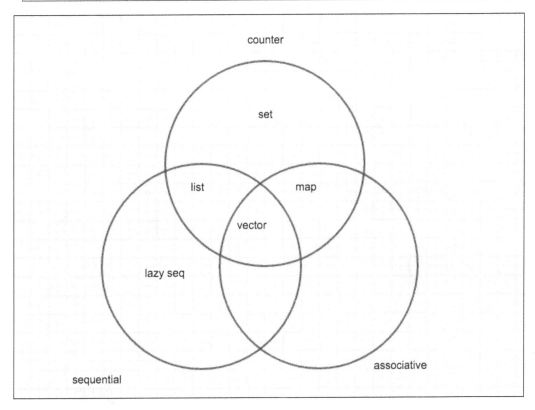

In the previous table and diagram, you can see that we take **Set** into account and as you can see, it's neither sequential nor associative.

We should look at another property; whether a collection is counted or not. It means that a collection knows how many elements it has. Lists, vectors, maps, and sets are all counted; lazy sequences are not counted, since they are generated on the fly and they could even be infinite sequences.

We will learn more about all of these sequences in the later sections of this chapter.

The sequence abstraction

Clojure has some unique features that make it different from other Lisps; one of them is the sequence abstraction. You can think of it as an interface that collections comply with. Clojure has a standard API of functions that you can use with sequences. Here are some examples of those functions:

- The `distinct` function: This function returns a sequence that includes each element of the original sequence just once:

  ```
  (def c [1 1 2 2 3 3 4 4 1 1])
  (distinct c)  ;; (1 2 3 4)
  ```

- The `take` function: This function takes a number of elements from the original sequence:

  ```
  (take 5 c)  ;; (1 1 2 2 3)
  ```

- The `map` function: This function applies a function to each element of a sequence and creates a new sequence with these elements:

  ```
  (map #(+ % 1) c)  ;; (2 2 3 3 4 4 5 5 2 2)
  ```

The interesting part here is that these functions receive and return sequences and you can compose them together. It can be seen in the following code:

```
(->> c
 (distinct)
 (take 5)
 (reverse))  ;; (4 3 2 1)

;; This is known as a threading macro, it applies distinct, then take
5 then reverse to the
;; collection c so this is the same as writing:
;; (reverse (take 5 (distinct c))) but much more readable
```

These are just some functions that accept and return sequences, but there are a lot more that you can use out of the box. The only assumption is that your sequence argument can respond to three functions:

- `first`: This function returns the first of a sequence
- `rest`: This function returns another sequence, containing everything but the first element
- `cons`: This function receives two parameters, an item and another `seq` and returns a new `seq` containing the item followed by all the items in the second parameter

 One of the functions that you'll find yourself using more is the `seq` function, it can convert any collection to a seq, even Java native arrays and objects that implement the `java.util.Iterable` interface. One of its main uses is to test a collection for emptiness.

Specific collection types in Clojure

Now that you know about Clojure's general collection properties and the sequence abstraction, it is a good time to get to know about Clojure's specific collection implementations.

Vectors

Vectors are Clojure's workhorse; together with map, it is the most used collection. Don't be afraid of them; they have nothing to do with Java's `java.util.Vector`. They are just a series of ordered values, such as a list or an array.

They have the following properties:

- They are immutable
- They can be accessed sequentially
- They are associative (they are maps of their indices, meaning that their keys are 0, 1, 2, and so on)
- They are counted, meaning they have a finite size
- They have random access, so you can access any element with almost constant time (with the nth function)
- The `conj` function appends a given element to them

The nth function allows us to get the nth element of any `seq`, but you shouldn't use it without care. It has no problem handling vectors and it returns in constant time, but it takes linear time when used with a list, since it has to traverse all the collections looking for the element you asked. Try to use it just with vectors.

They have a literal syntax; you can define a vector with square brackets, as shown:

```
[42 4 2 3 4 4 5 5]
```

Besides the literal syntax, there's another function that you can use to build a vector. The `vec` function can build a vector out of any sequence passed to it:

```
(vec (range 4)) ;; [0 1 2 3]
```

Another important benefit of vectors is that they are used for function arguments for declarations and for `let` bindings.

Take a look at the following example:

```
(def f [some-param & some-other-params] …)
```

```
(let [one 1 two (f p p-2 p-3)] …)
```

As you can see, the parameters in the function are defined as a vector, same as the `let` binding.

One of the main complaints about Lisps is that they use too many parentheses, Clojure's decision to use vectors instead in these structures is welcomed and makes the code much easier to read.

There are several ways to access a certain element of a vector:

- **Using the vector as a function**: Vectors can be used as functions of their keys; we haven't discussed maps yet but you will see that this is because they are associative:

  ```
  (def v [42 24 13 2 11 "a"])
  (v 0) ;; 42
  (v 99) ;; java.lang.IndexOutOfBoundsException
  ```

- **The nth function**: The `nth` function can receive an extra parameter for signaling when an index is not found and can be used, as shown:

  ```
  (nth v 0) ;; 42
  (nth v 99 :not-found) ;; :not-found
  (nth v 99) ;; java.lang.IndexOutOfBoundsException
  ```

- **The get function**: The `get` function can receive an extra parameter for signaling when an index is not found, it is used as shown. An important thing to keep in mind is that unlike nth, `get` cannot be used in sequences:

```
(get v 0)  ;; 42
(get v 99 :not-found)  ;; :not-found
(get v 99)  ;; nil
```

You should use vectors almost always; in particular, if you want to do any of the following there is no other way to go:

- You need random access to a collection (either modifying or accessing it)
- You need to add elements at the tail of the collection

Lists

Lists are the most important collection type in other Lisps. In Clojure, they are used to represent code, but their functionality is almost limited to that.

Lists in Clojure are single linked lists; as you can imagine, this means that they are not good for random access (you need to iterate the list until you get to the wanted index). That said, you can still use lists as sequences with every function of the API.

Let's list their properties:

- They are immutable
- They can be accessed sequentially
- They are not associative
- They are counted, meaning they have a finite size
- They shouldn't be accessed in random order. If you want the 99th element, then Clojure will have to visit all the first 98 elements to get the 99th.
- The `conj` function prepends a given element to it

You can use destructuring with lists, as seen in the previous chapter. You shouldn't be afraid to use the first function (or even nth with a small index).

 Lists have their use cases and as you learn more you'll probably be comfortable using them in some places (such as macros), but as a rule of thumb, try to use vectors instead.

Maps

Maps are probably the most important collection type across all languages. They are also very important in Clojure.

Maps are collections of key value pairs, which mean that you can access or store an element by a key. We have been calling this type of collection an associative collection. Keys can be of any type of value in Clojure, even functions, lists, sets, vectors, or other maps.

Sorted maps and hash maps

There are two types of maps in Clojure, each one of them with its own advantages.

- **Hash maps**: They are the most used form of map in Clojure; the literal syntax of maps creates this type of maps. They have a nearly constant lookup time, which makes them extremely fast and usable in most scenarios. Their downside is that you can't access them in an ordered fashion. You can create them, as shown:

  ```
  {:one 1 :two 2}
  (hash-map :one 1 :two 2)
  ```

- **Sorted maps**: If you need to be able to access a map's key-value pairs in a certain order, then you have to use a sorted map. The downside of sorted maps is that the lookup time is *not* constant, which means that they are a little slower to access by key. However, when you need to traverse a map in the order of the keys, then this is the only way to go. A strong constraint here is that the keys must be comparable between them. Sorted maps can be created, as shown:

  ```
  (sorted-map :sample 5 :map :6) ;; {:sample 5, :map 6}
  (sorted-map-by > 1 :one 5 :five 3 :three) ;; {5 :five, 3 :three, 1
  :one}
  ```

   Comparable objects are the ones that implement the compareTo interface.

Common properties

Associative objects, including maps have the following properties:

- They are functions of their keys:

```
(def m #{:one 1 :two 2 :three 3})
(m :one) ;; 1
(m 1) ;; nil
```

- They can be used with associative destructuring:

```
(let [{:keys [a b c d]} #{:a 5}]
  [a b]) ;
; [:a nil]
```

- They can be accessed with the get function:

```
(get m :one) ;; 1
(get m 1) ;; nil
(get m 1 :not-found) ;; :not-found
```

You can convert a map to a seq with the seq function; you will get a sequence where each element is a vector representing a key-value pair in the map:

```
(seq {:one 1 42 :forty-two :6 6}) ;; ([:one 1] [:6 6] [42 :forty-two])
(doseq [[k v] (seq {:one 1 42 :forty-two :6 6})]
  (println k v))
;; :one 1
;; :6 6
;; 42 :forty-two
```

Doseq is similar to Java's for-each loop. It executes the body for each element in a sequence.

It works as shown: (doseq [x sequence] ;;. This works the same way as the let statement, you can use destructuring if needed:

```
  (body-that-uses x))
```

Sets

Clojure sets are a collection of unique elements. You can think of them as mathematical sets and as such, Clojure has operations, such as union intersection and difference.

Let's look at the properties of sets:

- They are immutable
- They are associative (their keys are their elements)
- They are counted, meaning they have a finite size
- Their elements are unique (contained at most once)

Sorted sets and hash sets

There are two kinds of sets: hash-sets and sorted-sets.

- **Hash-set**: Besides the properties that we already saw, hash-sets are unordered. They are implemented using a hash map as a backing implementation.
- **Sorted-set**: Besides the properties that we already saw, sorted-sets are sorted. They can be used as a parameter to all the functions that expect a sorted `seq`. They can be accessed sequentially in sorted order:

```
(doseq [x (->> (sorted-set :b :c :d)
                (map name))]
    (println x))
;; b
;; c
;; d
```

You can also reverse them without problems, filter them, or map them similarly to a vector or list.

Common properties

Sets are associative, which gives them some properties of maps:

- They are functions of their elements:
  ```
  (#{:a :b :c :d} :a);; :a
  (#{:a :b :c :d} :e);; nil
  ```

- They can be used with map destructuring:
  ```
  (let [{:keys [b]} #{:b}] b);; :b
  (let [{:keys [c]} #{:b}] b);; nil
  (let [{:keys [c]} (sorted-set :b)] c);; nil
  (let [{:keys [b]} (sorted-set :b)] b);; :b
  ```

- The get function can be used to access their elements:

```
(get #{:a :b :c :d} :e :not-found) ;; :not-found
(get #{:a :b :c :d} :a) ;; :a
(get #{:a :b :c :d} :e) ;; nil
```

Union, difference, and intersection

If you remember mathematical sets, you'll know that the three main operations you can execute on them are the following:

- **Union** (union a b): The union includes all of the elements both in a and b
- **Difference** (difference a b): The difference is all the elements that are in a except for the elements that are also in b
- **Intersection** (intersection a b): It includes only the elements that are both in a and b

Here are some examples:

```
(def a #{:a :b :c :d :e})
(def b #{:a :d :h :i :j :k})

(require '[clojure.set :as s])

(s/union a b) ;; #{:e :k :c :j :h :b :d :i :a}
(s/difference a b) ;; #{:e :c :b}
(s/intersection a b) ;; #{:d :a}
```

Applying functional programming to collections

Now that we have a better understanding of how collections work, we have a better foundation to understand functional programming and how to make the most out of it.

This requires a different way of thinking about how to solve problems and you should keep your mind open.

Something that you might have found really strange about all of the collections is this feature: *They are immutable.*

This is indeed something quite strange; if you are used to Java, how can you possibly write programs without adding or removing elements from a list or set?

How is that even possible? In Java, we are used to writing `for` and `while` loops. We are used to mutating variables every step of the way.

How can we cope with immutable data structures? Let's find out in the subsequent sections.

The imperative programming model

The software industry has been using a single software paradigm for a long time; this paradigm is an imperative programming model.

In the imperative paradigm, you have to tell the computer what to do at every single step. You are responsible for how the memory works, for whether it is running in a single core or multi core and, if you want to use multi core, you need to make sure that you change the program state correctly and avoid concurrency problems.

Let's see how you would calculate the factorial in an imperative style:

```
int factorial(int n) {
    int result = 1;
    for (int i = 1; i <= n; i++) {
        result *= i;
    }
    return result;
}
```

You are creating a variable result and a variable `i`. You change the variable `i` each time by assigning it the value `i + 1`. You can change the result by multiplying by `i`. The computer just executes your orders, comparing, adding, and multiplying. This is what we call the imperative programming model, because you need to tell the computer the exact commands it needs to execute.

This has worked fine in the past for various reasons, such as:

- The tight constraints of memory size forced programmers to make use of the memory as efficient as possible
- It was easier to think about a single thread of execution and how the computer executes it step-by-step

Of course, there were some drawbacks. A code can get complicated easily and the world has changed; the constraints that existed many years ago are gone. In addition, most of today's computers have more than one CPU. Multi-threading with shared mutable states is burdensome.

This makes thinking about this complicated. We get in trouble even in single threaded programs; just think, what would be the outcome of the following code?

```
List l = new ArrayList();
doSomething(l);
System.out.println(l.size());
```

Is it 0? You can't possibly know because the doSomething method gets the list by reference and it can add or remove things without you knowing.

Now, imagine that you have a multithreaded program and a single List that can be modified by any of the threads. In the Java world, you have to know about java.util.concurrent.CopyOnWriteArrayList and you need to know about its implementation details to know when it's a good idea to use it and when not to use it.

Even with these structures, it is difficult to think about multithreaded code. You still need to think about semaphores, locks, synchronizers, and so on.

The imperative world might be easy for the easy case, but it is not simple. The whole industry has realized this and there are many new languages and technologies that take ideas from other places. Java 8 has the streaming API and it includes lambda blocks, which are essentially functions. All these ideas are taken from the functional world.

The functional paradigm

There are other ways of thinking about how to solve a problem; in particular, the functional paradigm has become important lately. It is nothing new; Lisp has supported this kind of programming since it was conceived in 1958. It has probably not been strong until recently, as it requires a more abstract way of thinking.

For you to get a better idea, let's see a couple of examples of how functional programming looks similar to the following code:

```
(map str [1 2 3 4 5 6]) ;; ("1" "2" "3" "4" "5" "6")

(defn factorial [n]
  (reduce * (range 1 (inc n))))

(factorial 5) ;; 120
```

As you can see, it looks quite different; in the first case, we are passing the str function to another function called map.

In the second case, we are passing the * function to another function called reduce. In both cases, we are using functions as you would pass a list or a number, they are **first level citizens**.

One important difference in functional programming is that you don't need to tell the machine how to do things. In the first case, the map traverses the vector and applies the str function to each element, converting it to a seq of strings. You don't have to increment the index, you just need to tell the map what function you want to be applied to each element.

In the factorial case, there is a reduce function that receives the * and a seq from 1 to n.

It just works, you don't need to tell it how to do anything, just what you want done.

Both map and reduce are **higher order functions** because they accept functions such as parameters; they are also higher level abstractions.

 Higher order functions are functions that either accept a function as an argument, return a function as result, or both.

You need to think on another level of abstraction and you don't care how things are really done, just that it gets the work done.

This comes with some benefit, if the implementation of a map someday changes to become multithreaded, you would just need to update the versions and you would be ready to go!

Functional programming and immutability

You may have also noticed that functional programming makes working with immutable structures necessary, because you can't mutate some or the other state in every step; you can just describe how you want to create a new collection based on some other collection and then get it. Clojure's efficient collections make it possible to share pieces of collections to keep memory usage at a minimum.

There are some other benefits to immutability:

- You can share your data structures with anyone you want because you are certain that nobody can change your copy.

- Debugging is simpler because you can test the program with some immutable value instead of some mutating state. When you get a value, you can find out which function returned the value that you got; there are not multiple places where a collection was mutated for you to check.

- Concurrent programming is simpler; again being certain that nobody can change your copy, even in other concurrently running threads, makes reasoning about your program simpler.

Laziness

Clojure also supports lazy evaluation of transformations of sequences. Let's take a look at the `range` function:

```
(def r (range))
```

When running this function without parameters, you are creating an infinite sequence starting from `0`.

It is an infinite sequence; so why does the Clojure REPL return automatically?

Clojure doesn't compute a collection value until needed, so in order to get a value you would have to do something, such as this:

```
(take 1 r);; (0)
(take 5 r);; (0 1 2 3 4)
```

 If you try to print an infinite sequence at the REPL, it will freeze.

Here, Clojure is resolving first one element and then five of the collection `r` because it needs to print them in the REPL.

 Lazy evaluation just works for collections and for sequence processing. Other operations (such as additions, method calls, and so on), are executed eagerly.

The interesting part is that you can define a new lazy collection by applying functions like filter and map to a certain collection.

For instance, let's get a new collection that contains all odd numbers:

```
(def odd-numbers (filter odd? r))
(take 1 odd-numbers)   ;; (1)
(take 2 odd-numbers)   ;; (1 3)
(take 3 odd-numbers)   ;; (1 3 5)
```

Now, odd-numbers is an infinite sequence of odd numbers and we have just asked for three of them. Whenever a number is already computed, it is not computed again. Let's change our collection a little bit in order to understand how this works:

```
(defn logging-odd? [number]
    (println number) ;; This is terrible, it is a side effect and
    a source for problems
                     ;; Clojure encourages you to avoid side
     effects, but it is pragmatic
                     ;; and relies on you knowing what you are
    doing
    (odd? number))

(def odd-numbers (filter logging-odd? r))

(take 1 odd-numbers)
;; 0
;; 1
;; 2
;; 3
;; 4
;; 5
;; 6
;; 7
;; 8
;; 9
;; 10
;; 11
;; 12
;; 13
;; 14
;; 15
;; 16
;; 17
;; 18
;; 19
;; 20
;; 21
;; 22
;; 23
;; 24
;; 25
;; 26
;; 27
;; 28
;; 29
;; 30
;; 31
;; => (1)
```

```
(take 1 odd-numbers)
;; => (1)

(take 2 odd-numbers)
;; => (1 3)

(take 3 odd-numbers)
;; => (1 3 5)

(take 4 odd-numbers)
;; => (1 3 5 7)

(take 10 odd-numbers)
;; => (1 3 5 7 9 11 13 15 17 19)
```

As you can see, some numbers get calculated first; you shouldn't expect or rely on a particular number of elements to be precomputed at a certain time.

Also, keep in mind that the computation isn't executed again when we ask for the same number of elements, since it has been already cached.

Summary

Collections and functional programming in Clojure are extremely powerful tools that allow us to use a completely different paradigm of programming.

Here's what we have learned so far:

- The mechanics of immutable collections and what each collection type in Clojure is best for

- How sequence abstraction and how a lot of Clojure functions are available to work on collections, using this abstraction

- How functional programming enables us to write simpler programs that work better in parallel environments and help us save resources using laziness

In the subsequent chapters, we will learn about other new Clojure features that give us a new and much more powerful way to implement polymorphism than what Java offers.

5
Multimethods and Protocols

We now have a better understanding of how Clojure works; we understand how to perform simple operations with immutable data structures but we are missing some features that could make our lives much easier.

If you have been a Java programmer for a while, you are probably thinking about polymorphism and its particular flavor in Java.

Polymorphism is one of the concepts that enable us to reuse a code. It gives us the ability to interact with different objects with the same API.

Clojure has a powerful polymorphism paradigm that allows us to write simple code, create code that interacts with types that don't exist yet, and extend code in ways it wasn't devised for when a programmer wrote it.

To help us with polymorphism in Clojure, we have two important concepts that we will cover in this chapter:

- Multimethods
- Protocols

Each of them has its own use cases and things it is best at; we will look into them in the next section.

We will learn each of these different concepts by reviewing what we already know from Java and then we will learn similar concepts from Clojure that give us much more power.

Polymorphism in Java

Java uses polymorphism heavily, its collection API is based on it. Probably the best examples of polymorphism in Java are the following classes:

- `java.util.List`
- `java.util.Map`
- `java.util.Set`

We know that depending on our use case we should use a particular implementation of these data structures.

If we prefer to use an ordered Set, we might use a TreeSet.

If we need a Map in a concurrent environment, we will use a `java.util.concurrent.ConcurrentHashMap`.

The beautiful thing is that you can write your code using the `java.util.Map` and `java.util.Set` interfaces and if you need to change to another type of Set or Map, because the conditions have changed or someone has created a better version of the collection for you, you don't need to change any code!

Lets look at a very simple example of polymorphism in Java.

Imagine that you have a Shapes hierarchy; it might look similar to the following code:

```
package shapes;

public interface Shape {
  public double getArea();
}

public class Square implements Shape {
  private double side;
  public Square(double side) {
this.side = side;
  }

  public double getArea() {
    return side * side;
  }
```

```
}

public class Circle implements Shape {
  private double radius;
  public Circle(double radius) {
this.radius = radius;
  }

  public double getArea() {
    return Math.PI * radius * radius;
  }

}
```

You surely are aware of the power of this concept, you can now calculate the summation of all the areas of a collection of figures, such as this:

```
package shapes;

import java.util.List;
import java.util.Arrays;

public class Main {

  public static double totalArea(List<Shape> shapes) {

    double result = 0;
    for(Shape s : shapes) {
      result += s.getArea();
    }

    return result;
  }

  public static void main(String args[]) {
    System.out.println(totalArea(Arrays.asList(new Circle(5), new Square(3), new Circle(4.5))));
  }
}
```

The totalArea method doesn't care about the specific types of shapes that you pass to it and you can add new types of shapes, such as rectangles or trapezoids. Your same code will now work with new data types.

Now, with the same Java code base, imagine that you wanted to add a new function to your shape interface, something simple, such as a getPerimeter method.

This seems quite simple; you will have to modify each class that implements the Shape interface. I'm sure you've faced this problem a lot of times when you don't have access to the base source. The solution is to write a wrapper around your Shape objects but this introduces more classes and incidental complexity.

Clojure has its own idea of polymorphism, it is much simpler but also very powerful; you can in fact solve the perimeter problem with it in a very simple way.

One way to solve this is with multimethods; lets have a look at how they work.

Multimethods in Clojure

Multimethods are similar to interfaces, they allow you to write a common contract and then a family of functions can fulfill that interface with a specific implementation.

They are extremely flexible, as you will see they grant you a very fine control over what function is going to get invoked for a specific data object.

Multimethods consist of three parts:

- A function (or method) declaration
- A dispatch function
- Each possible implementation of the function

One of the most interesting features of multimethods is that you can implement new functions for already existing types without having to write wrappers around your currently existing object.

The multimethod declaration works the same way as the interface; you define a common contract for the polymorphic function, as shown:

```
(defmulti name docstring? attr-map? dispatch-fn& options)
```

The `defmulti` macro defines the contract for your multimethod, it consists of:

- The multimethod's name
- An optional `docstring` (this is the documentation string)
- The attribute map
- The `dispatch-fn` function

> The `dispatch` function gets called for every piece of content; it generates a dispatch key that is later checked against its function implementation. When the dispatch key and the key in the function implementation match, the function is called.

The `dispatch` function receives the same parameters that the function you are calling receives and returns a dispatch key that is used to determine the function that should dispatch the request.

Each implementation function must define a dispatch key, if it matches with the `dispatch` function's result, then this function is executed.

An example should clarify:

```
(defmulti area :shape)

(defmethod area :square [{:keys [side]}] (* side side))

(area {:shape :square :side 5})
;;=> 25
```

Here, we are defining a multimethod called `area`; the `defmulti` statement has the following structure:

```
(defmulti function-name dispatch-function)
```

In this case, the multimethod is called `area` and the `dispatch` function is the `:shape` keyword.

> Remember, keywords can be used as functions that look up themselves in maps. So, for example, the result of (`:shape` {`:shape` `:square`}) is `:square`.

Afterwards, we define a method, as shown:

```
(defmethod function-name dispatch-key [params] function-body)
```

Note that the `dispatch-key` is always the result of invoking the `dispatch-function` with `params` as parameters.

Finally, let's look at the invocation, `(area {:shape :square :side 5})` which is calling a multimethod. The first thing that happens is that we call the dispatch function `:shape`, as shown:

```
(:shape {:shape :square :side 5})
;; :square
```

The `:square` function is now the dispatch key, we need to look for the method that has that dispatch key; in this case, the only method that we defined works. So, the function is executed and we get the result of 25.

It is pretty simple to add the area and perimeter for both square and circle, lets check the implementation:

```
(defmethodarea :circle [{:keys [radius]}]
(* Math/PI radius radius))

(defmultiperimeter :shape)

(defmethodperimeter :square [{:keys [side]}] (* side 4))

(defmethodperimeter :circle [{:keys [radius]}] (* 2 Math/PI radius))
```

Now, we have defined how to calculate the perimeter and area of circles and squares with very little effort and without having to define a very strict object hierarchy. However, we are just starting to uncover the power of multimethods.

Keywords can be namespaced, it allows you to keep your code better organized. There are two ways to define a namespaced keyword, such as `:namespace/keyword` and `::keyword`. When using the `::` notation, the used namespace is the current namespace. So if you write `::test` in the REPL, you will be defining `:user/test`.

Let's try another example, copy the following code into your REPL:

```
user=> (defmulti walk :type)
#'user/walk
user=>

user=> (defmethod walk ::animal [_] "Just walk")
#object[clojure.lang.MultiFn 0x58c715bf "clojure.lang.MultiFn@58c715bf"]
user=> (defmethod walk ::primate [_] "Primate walk")
#object[clojure.lang.MultiFn 0x58c715bf "clojure.lang.MultiFn@58c715bf"]
user=> (walk {:type ::animal})
"Just walk"
user=>

user=> (walk {:type ::primate})
"Primate walk"
user=>
```

As you can see, it just works as you might expect it to. However, let's see how you can create a keyword hierarchy to be a little bit more flexible than this.

Keyword hierarchies

You can declare that a keyword derives from another keyword and then respond to other dispatch keys, for that you can use the `derive` function:

```
(derive ::hominid ::primate)
```

 When defining a keyword hierarchy, you have to use namespaced keywords.

Here, you are declaring that the ::hominid key is derived from the ::animal key
and you can now use ::hominid as ::animal; let's see that now:

```
(walk {:type ::hominid})
;; Primate Walk
```

We do have some problems when defining hierarchies, for instance what will
happen if the same keyword were to be derived from two conflicting keywords?
Let's give it a try:

```
(derive ::hominid ::animal)
```

```
(walk {:type ::hominid})
;;java.lang.IllegalArgumentException: Multiple methods in multimethod
'walk' match dispatch value: :boot.user/hominid -> :boot.user/animal
and :boot.user/primate, and neither is preferred
```

We get an error that says, there are two methods that match the dispatch value.
Since our hominid derives both from animal and primate, it doesn't know which
to resolve.

We can work this out explicitly with:

```
(prefer-method walk ::hominid ::primate)
(walk {:type ::hominid})
; Primate walk
```

Now, everything works correctly. We know that we prefer to resolve to a primate
when calling the walk multimethod with the hominid key.

You can also define a more specific method, just for the hominid key:

```
(defmethodwalk ::hominid [_] "Walk in two legs")
```

```
(walk {:type ::hominid})
;; Walk in two legs
```

The derivation hierarchy can get a little complex and we might need some functions
to introspect relationships. Clojure has the following functions to work with
type hierarchies.

- isa?
- parents
- descendants
- underive

isa?

The isa function checks if a type derives from some other type, it works with Java classes as well as Clojure keywords.

It is simple to explain with examples:

```
(isa? java.util.ArrayListjava.util.List)
;;=> true

(isa? ::hominid ::animal)
;;=> true

(isa? ::animal ::primate)
;;=> false
```

parents

The parent function returns a set of a type's parents, they might be Java or Clojure keywords:

```
(parents java.util.ArrayList)
;;=> #{java.io.Serializablejava.util.Listjava.lang.Cloneablejava.util.
RandomAccessjava.util.AbstractList}

(parents ::hominid)
#{:user/primate :user/animal}
```

descendants

The descendants function, as you can imagine, returns a set of descendants of the passd keyword; it is important to keep in mind that in this case only Clojure keywords are allowed:

```
(descendants ::animal)
;;=> #{:boot.user/hominid}
```

underive

The underive function breaks the relation between two types, as you can imagine it only works with the Clojure keywords:

```
(underive ::hominid ::animal)
;;=> (isa? ::hominid ::animal)
```

This function will normally be used at development time and they allow you to play around with your type hierarchy in a very simple and dynamic way.

A la carte dispatch functions

Until now, we have used a keyword as a dispatch function but you can use any function you like with as many arguments as you want. Let's take a look at some examples:

```
(defn dispatch-func [arg1 arg2]
  [arg2 arg1])
```

This is a simple function, but it shows two important facts:

- The dispatch function can receive more than one argument
- The dispatch key can be anything, not just a keyword

Lets have a look at how we can use this dispatch function:

```
(defmulti sample-multimethod dispatch-func)
;; Here we are saying that we want to use dispatch-func to calculate
the dispatch-key

(defmethod sample-multimethod [:second :first] [first second]
[:normal-params first second])
(defmethod sample-multimethod [:first :second] [first second]
[:switch-params second first])

(sample-multimethod :first :second)
;;=> [:normal-params :first: second]

(sample-multimethod :second :first)
;; =>[:switch-params :first: second]
```

We are getting to know the dispatch function a little bit better; now that you know that you can implement any dispatch function, you have a very fine grained control over what function gets called and when.

Lets look at one more example, so we can finally grasp the complete idea:

```
user=> (defn avg [& coll]
  #_=>    (/ (apply + coll) (count coll)))
#'user/avg
user=> (defn get-race [& ages]
  #_=>    (if (> (apply avg ages) 120)
  #_=>       :timelord
  #_=>       :human))
#'user/get-race
user=> (defmulti travel get-race)
#'user/travel
user=>

user=> (defmethod travel :timelord [&  ages]
  #_=>    (str (count ages) " timelords travelling by tardis"))
#object[clojure.lang.MultiFn 0x6cc1d65c "clojure.lang.MultiFn@6cc1d65c"]
user=> (defmethod travel :human [&  ages]
  #_=>    (str (count ages) " humans travelling by car"))
#object[clojure.lang.MultiFn 0x6cc1d65c "clojure.lang.MultiFn@6cc1d65c"]
user=> (travel 2000 1000 100 200)
"4 timelords travelling by tardis"
user=> (travel 80 20 100 40)
"4 humans travelling by car"
user=>
```

Now the true power of multimethods becomes apparent. You now have an adhoc way of defining polymorphic functions which has the possibility to define type hierarchies and even execute your own logic to determine the function that is going to be called finally.

Protocols in Clojure

Multimethods are just one of the options for polymorphism you have in Clojure, there are other ways to implement polymorphic functions.

Protocols are a little easier to understand and they might feel more similar to Java interfaces.

Lets try to define our shape program using protocols:

```
(defprotocol Shape
  "This is a protocol for shapes"
  (perimeter [this] "Calculates the perimeter of this shape")
  (area [this] "Calculates the area of this shape"))
```

Here, we have defined a protocol and it is called shaped and everything that implements this protocol must implement the following two functions: `perimeter` and `area`.

There are a number of ways to implement a protocol; one interesting feature is that you can even extend Java classes to implement a protocol without an access to the Java source and without having to recompile anything.

Let's start by creating a record that implements the type.

Records in Clojure

Records work exactly like maps, but they are much faster if you stick to the predefined keys. Defining a record is similar to defining a class, Clojure knows beforehand about the fields that the record will have, so it can generate byte code on the fly and the code that uses the records is much faster.

Lets define a `Square` record, as shown:

```
(defrecord Square [side]
  Shape
  (perimeter [{:keys [side]}] (* 4 side))
  (area [{:keys [side]}] (* side side)))
```

Here, we are defining the `Square` record and it has the following properties:

- It has only one field, `size`; this is going to work as a map with only the side key
- It implements the `Shape` protocol

Lets have a look at how a record is instantiated and how we can use it:

```
(Square. 5)
;;=> #user/Square{:size 5}

(def square (Square. 5))

(let [{side :side} square] side)
;;=> 5

(let [{:keys [side]} square] side)
;;=> 5

(doseq [[k v] (Square. 5)] (println k v))
;; :side 5
```

As you can see it works exactly like a map, you can even associate things to it:

```
(assoc (Square. 5) :hello :world)
```

The downside of doing this is that we no longer have the performance guarantees that we had when defining just the record fields; nonetheless, it is a great way of giving some structure to our code.

We still have to check how we can use our perimeter and area functions, it is pretty simple. Let's have a look:

```
(perimeter square)
;;=> 20

(area square)
;;=> 25
```

Just to continue with the example, let's define the `Circle` record:

```
(defrecord Circle [radius]
  Shape
  (perimeter [{:keys [radius]}] (* Math/PI 2 radius))
  (area [{:keys [radius]}] (* Math/PI radius radius)))

(def circle (Circle. 5))
```

```
(perimeter circle)
;;=> 31.41592653589793

(area circle)
;;=> 78.53981633974483
```

One of the promises was that we will be able to extend our existing records and types without having to touch the current code. Well, lets keep to that promise and check how to extend our records without having to touch existing code.

Imagine, we need to add a predicate telling us whether a shape has an area or not; we might then define the next protocol, as shown:

```
(defprotocolShapeProperties
  (num-sides [this] "How many sides a shape has"))
```

Let's get directly to the extend type, which is going to help us define this `num-sides` function for our old protocols. Note that with `extend-type` we can even define functions for existing Java types:

```
(extend-type Square
ShapeProperties
  (num-sides [this] 4))

(extend-type Circle
ShapeProperties
  (num-sides [this] Double/POSITIVE_INFINITY))

(num-sides square)
;;=> 4

(num-sides circle)
;;=> Infinity
```

Protocols become much more interesting when you extend them for Java types. Lets create a protocol that includes some functions for list like structures:

```
(defprotocolListOps
  (positive-values [list])
  (negative-values [list])
  (non-zero-values [list]))
```

```
(extend-type java.util.List
ListOps
  (positive-values [list]
    (filter #(> % 0) list))
  (negative-values [list]
    (filter #(< % 0) list))
  (non-zero-values [list]
    (filter #(not= % 0) list)))
```

And now you can use the positive values, negative values and `non-zero-values` with anything that extends from `java.util.List`, including Clojure's vectors:

```
(positive-values [-1 0 1])
;;=> (1)

(negative-values [-1 0 1])
;;=> (-1)

(no-zero-values [-1 0 1])
;;=> (-1 1)
```

It might not be very exciting to extend `java.util.List`, since you can define these three as functions and it works the same way but you can extend any custom Java type with this mechanism.

Summary

Now we understand Clojure's way a little bit better and we have a better grasp of what to look for when we need polymorphism. We understand that when needing a polymorphic function we have several options:

- We can implement multimethods if we need a highly customized dispatching mechanism
- We can implement multimethods if we need to define a complex inheritance structure
- We can implement a protocol and define a custom type that implements that protocol
- We can define a protocol and extend existing Java or Clojure types with our custom functions for each type

Polymorphism in Clojure is very powerful. It allows you to extend the functionality of Clojure or Java types that already exist; it feels like adding methods to an interface. The best thing about it is that you don't need to redefine or recompile anything.

In the next chapter, we will talk about concurrency — one of the key features of Clojure. We will learn about the idea of what the identity and values are and how those key concepts make writing concurrent programs much easier.

6
Concurrency

Programming has changed, in the past we could just rely on computers getting faster year after year. This is proving to be more and more difficult; so, hardware manufacturers are taking a different approach. Now, they are embedding more processors into computers. Nowadays, it's not uncommon to see phones with just or four cores.

This calls for a different way of writing software, one in which we are able to execute some tasks in other processes, explicitly. The modern languages are trying to make this task feasible and easier for modern developers, and Clojure is no exception.

In this chapter, we will see how Clojure enables you to write simple concurrent programs by reviewing Clojure's core concepts and primitives; in particular, we need to understand the concept of identity and value that Clojure has embedded into the language. In this chapter, we will cover the following topics:

- Using your Java knowledge
- The Clojure model of state and identity
- Promises
- Futures
- Software transactional memory and refs
- Atoms
- Agents
- Validators
- Watchers

Using your Java knowledge

Knowing Java and your way around Java's threading APIs gives you a great advantage, since Clojure relies on the tools that you already know.

Here, you'll see how to use threads and you can extend everything you see here to execute other services.

Before going any further, let's create a new project that we'll use as a sandbox for all of our tests.

Create it, as shown in the following screenshot:

```
# iamedu at Eduardos-MacBook-Pro.local in ~ [5:23:35]
$ lein new clojure-concurrency
Generating a project called clojure-concurrency based on the 'default' template.
The default template is intended for library projects, not applications.
To see other templates (app, plugin, etc), try `lein help new`.
```

Modify the `clojure-concurrency.core` namespace, so that it looks similar to the following code snippet:

```clojure
(ns clojure-concurrency.core)

(defn start-thread [func]
  (.start (Thread. func)))
```

It's easy to understand what's happening here. We are creating a thread with our function and then starting it; so that we can use it in the REPL, as follows:

```
clojure-concurrency.core=> (require 'clojure-concurrency.core :reload-all)
WARNING: await already refers to: #'clojure.core/await in namespace: clojure-concurrency.core, being replaced by: #'co.paralleluniverse.pul
sar.core/await
WARNING: promise already refers to: #'clojure.core/promise in namespace: clojure-concurrency.core, being replaced by: #'co.paralleluniverse
.pulsar.core/promise
WARNING: test already refers to: #'clojure.core/test in namespace: clojure-concurrency.core, being replaced by: #'clojure-concurrency.core/
test
nil
clojure-concurrency.core=> (in-ns 'clojure-concurrency.core)
#object[clojure.lang.Namespace 0x736fc8a0 "clojure-concurrency.core"]
clojure-concurrency.core=> (start-thread #(println "Hello threaded world"))
Hello threaded world
nil
```

> `java.lang.Thread` has a constructor, which receives an object implementing the runnable interface. You can just pass a Clojure function because every function in Clojure implements runnable and callable interfaces. This means that you can also use the executors transparently in Clojure!

We'll see a `nil` and `Hello threaded world` values in any random order. The `nil` value is what the start thread returns.

The `Hello threaded world` is a message from another thread. With this, we now have the basic tools to get to know and understand how threads work in Clojure.

The Clojure model of state and identity

Clojure has very strong opinions about concurrency, in order to take it in a simpler way it redefines what state and identity mean. Let's explore the meaning of this concepts in Clojure.

When talking about state in Java, you probably think about the values of the attributes of your Java classes. The state in Clojure is similar to Java, it refers to the values of objects but there are very important differences that allow simpler concurrency.

In Clojure, identity is an entity that might have different values over time. Consider the following examples:

- I have an identity; I will be and continue being this particular individual, my opinions, ideas, and appearance might change over time but I am the same individual with the same identity.

- You have a bank account; it has a particular number and is run by a particular bank. The amount of money you have in it changes over time, but it is the same bank account.

- Consider a ticker symbol (such as GOOG), it identifies a stock in the stock market; the value associated with it changes over time, but not its identity.

State is a value that an identity took at some point in time. One of its important features is that it is immutable. State is a snapshot of an identity's value at some given time.

So, in the previous examples:

- Who you are right now, how you feel, how you look, and what you think is your current state

- The money you currently have in your bank account is its current state

- The value of the GOOG stock is its current state

All of these states are immutable; it doesn't matter who you are tomorrow or how much you win or spend. It is true and it will always be true that in this particular moment in time you have a certain state.

Rich Hickey, Clojure's author, is a great talker and has several talks in which he explains the ideas and philosophy behind Clojure. In one of them, (Are We There Yet?) he explains this idea of state, identity, and time very extensively.

Let's now explain the two key concepts in Clojure:

- **Identity**: Throughout your whole life, you have a single identity; you never stop being you, even if you keep changing throughout your whole life.

- **State**: At any given moment in your life, you are a certain person with likes, dislikes, and some beliefs. We call this way of being at a moment of your life, the state. If you look at a particular moment in your life, you will see a fixed value. Nothing will change the fact that you were the way you were in that moment in time. That particular state is immutable; over time, you have different states or values, but each of those states is immutable.

We use this fact to write simpler concurrent programs. Whenever you want to interact with an identity, you look at it and you get its current value (a snapshot at the time), and then you operate with what you have.

In imperative programming, you normally have a guarantee that you have the latest value but it is very difficult to keep it in a consistent state. The reason for this is that you are relying on a shared mutable state.

A shared mutable state is the reason why you need to use a synchronized code, locks, and mutexes. It is also the reason for very complex programs, with difficult bugs to track.

Nowadays, Java is learning the lessons from other programming languages and now it has primitives that allow simpler concurrent programming. These ideas are taken from other languages and newer ideas, so there is a good chance that someday you'll see similar concepts to what you'll study here in other mainstream programming languages.

There is no guarantee that you'll always have the latest value, but don't worry, you just have to think about things differently and use the concurrency primitives that Clojure gives you.

This is similar to how you work in real life, you don't know exactly what's happening with all of your friends or co-workers when you do something for them; you talk to them, get the current facts, and then go and get working. While you are at it, something needs to change; in this case we need a coordination mechanism.

Clojure has various such coordination mechanisms, let's have a look at them.

Promises

If you are a full stack Java developer, there is a good chance that you have met promises in JavaScript.

Promises are simple abstractions that don't impose strict requirements on you; you can use them to calculate the result on some other thread, light process, or anything you like.

In Java, there are a couple of ways to achieve this; one of them is with futures (`java.util.concurrentFuture`) and if you want something more similar to JavaScript's promise there is a nice implementation called **jdeferred** (`https://github.com/jdeferred/jdeferred`), which you might have used before.

In essence a promise is just a promise that you can give to your caller, the caller can use it at any given time. There are two possibilities:

- If the promise has already been fulfilled, the call returns immediately
- If not, the caller will block until the promise is fulfilled

Let's take a look at an example; remember to use the start-thread function in the `clojure-concurrency.core` package:

```
clojure-concurrency.core=> (in-ns 'clojure-concurrency.core)
#object[clojure.lang.Namespace 0x736fc8a0 "clojure-concurrency.core"]
clojure-concurrency.core=> (def p (promise))
#'clojure-concurrency.core/p
clojure-concurrency.core=> (start-thread
                #_=>    #(do
                #_=>       (deref p)
                #_=>       (println "Hello world")))
nil
```

 Promises are only calculated once and then cached. So don't worry about using them as many times as you like once it has been calculated, there is no runtime cost associated!

Let's stop here and analyze the code, we are creating a promise called `p` and then we start a thread that does two things.

It tries to get a value from `p` (the `deref` function tries to read the value from a promise) and then prints `Hello world`.

We won't see the `Hello world` message just yet; we will instead see a `nil` value. Why is that?

The start thread returns the `nil` value and what happens now is what we described in the first place; `p` is the promise and our new thread will block it until it gets a value.

In order to see the `Hello world` message, we need to deliver the promise. Let's do that now:

```
clojure-concurrency.core=> (deliver p 5)
Hello world
#object[co.paralleluniverse.pulsar.core$promise$reify__2871 0x6459f6f {:status :ready, :val 5}]
```

As you can see, we now get the `Hello world` message!

As I said, there is no need to use another thread. Let's now see another example in the REPL:

```
clojure-concurrency.core=> (def p (promise))
#'clojure-concurrency.core/p
clojure-concurrency.core=> (deliver p 5)
#object[co.paralleluniverse.pulsar.core$promise$reify__2871 0x68ead4cd {:status :ready, :val 5}]
clojure-concurrency.core=> @p
5
clojure-concurrency.core=> (println "Hello world")
Hello world
nil
```

 You can use @p instead of (`deref p`), it works for every identity in this chapter too.

In this example we don't create separate threads; we create the promise, deliver it, and then use it in the same thread.

As you can see, promises are an extremely simple type of synchronization mechanism, you can decide whether to use threads, executor services (which are just thread pools), or some other mechanism, such as lightweight threads.

Let's have a look at Pulsar library for creating lightweight threads.

Pulsar and lightweight threads

Creating a thread is an expensive operation and it consumes RAM memory. To know how much memory creating a thread consumes in Mac OS X or Linux, run the next command:

```
java -XX:+PrintFlagsFinal -version | grep ThreadStackSize
```

What you see here will depend on the OS and JVM version that you are using, with Java 1.8u45 on Mac OS X, we get the following output:

```
# iamedu at Eduardos-MacBook-Pro.local in ~/Development/clj/images/chapter06 [5:40:28]
$ java -XX:+PrintFlagsFinal -version | grep ThreadStackSize

    intx CompilerThreadStackSize         = 0            {pd product}
    intx ThreadStackSize                 = 1024         {pd product}
    intx VMThreadStackSize               = 1024         {pd product}
java version "1.8.0_66"
Java(TM) SE Runtime Environment (build 1.8.0_66-b17)
Java HotSpot(TM) 64-Bit Server VM (build 25.66-b17, mixed mode)
```

I am getting a stack size of 1024 kilobytes per thread. What can we do to improve the numbers? Other languages, such as Erlang and Go create a few threads from the beginning and then execute their tasks using those threads. It becomes important to be able to suspend a particular task and run another in the same thread.

In Clojure there is a library called **Pulsar** (https://github.com/puniverse/pulsar), which is an interface for a Java API called **Quasar** (https://github.com/puniverse/quasar).

In order to support Pulsar, as of version 0.6.2, you need to do two things.

- Add the [co.paralleluniverse/pulsar "0.6.2"] dependency to your project
- Add an instrumentation agent to your JVM (adding :java-agents [[co.paralleluniverse/quasar-core "0.6.2"]] to your project.clj)

The instrumentation agent should be able to suspend functions in a thread and then change them for other functions. In the end, your project.clj file should look similar to:

```
(defproject clojure-concurrency "0.1.0-SNAPSHOT"
 :description "FIXME: write description"
 :url "http://example.com/FIXME"
 :license {:name "Eclipse Public License"
           :url "http://www.eclipse.org/legal/epl-v10.html"}
           :dependencies [[org.clojure/clojure "1.6.0"]
           [co.paralleluniverse/pulsar "0.6.2"]]
 :java-agents [[co.paralleluniverse/quasar-core "0.6.2"]])
```

Let's write our last example with promises using Pulsar's lightweight threads called fibers.

Pulsar comes with its own promises in the `co.paralleluniverse.pulsar.core` package and they can be used as a drop-in replacement for promises in `clojure.core`:

```
(clojure.core/use 'co.paralleluniverse.pulsar.core)
(def p1 (promise))
(def p2 (promise))
(def p3 (promise))
(spawn-fiber #(clojure.core/deliver p2 (clojure.core/+ @p1 5)))
(spawn-fiber #(clojure.core/deliver p3 (clojure.core/+ @p1 @p2)))
(spawn-thread #(println @p3))
(clojure.core/deliver p1 99)
;; 203
```

This example is a bit more interesting, we use two of Pulsar's functions:

- `spawn-fiber`: This function creates a light thread, you can create thousands of fibers if you want in a single program. They are cheap to create and as long as you program them carefully, there shouldn't be many problems coming from this.

- `span-thread`: This is Pulsar's version of start-thread, it creates a real thread and runs it.

In this particular example, we calculate p2 and p3 in two fibers and then p3 in a thread. At this point, everything is waiting for us to deliver the value of p1; we do it with the `deliver` function.

Pulsar has other very interesting features that allow for simpler parallel programming, have a look at the documentation if you are interested. In the last part of this chapter, we will have a look at `core.async`. Pulsar has an interface modelled after `core.async`, which you can use if you like.

Futures

If you have been using Java for a while, you might know the `java.util.concurrent.Future` class, this is Clojure's implementation of futures and it is extremely similar to Java, only a bit simpler. Its interface and usage are almost identical to promises with a very important difference, when using futures everything will run in a different thread automatically.

Let's see a simple example using futures, in any REPL do the following:

```
(def f (future (Thread/sleep 20000) "Hello world"))
(println @f)
```

Your REPL should freeze for 20 seconds and then print `Hello world`.

> Futures are also cached, so you only need to pay once for the cost of calculation and then you can use them any number of times you want.

At first glance, futures look much easier than promises. You don't need to worry about creating threads or fibers, but there are downsides to this approach:

- You have less flexibility; you can only run futures in a predefined thread pool.

- You should be careful if your futures take too much time, they could end up NOT running because the implicit thread pool has a number of threads available. If they are all busy some of your tasks will end up queued and waiting.

`Futures` have their use cases, if you have very few processor intensive tasks, if you have IO bound tasks, maybe using promises with fibers is a good idea, since they allow you to keep your processor free to run more tasks concurrently.

Software transactional memory and refs

One of Clojure's most interesting features is **software transactional memory (STM)**. It uses **multiversion concurrency control (MVCC)**, in a very similar fashion to how databases work, implementing a form of optimistic concurrency control.

> MVCC is what databases use for transactions; what this means is that every operation within a transaction has its own copy of variables. After executing its operations, it checks if any of the used variables changed during the transaction and if they did the transaction fails. This is called optimistic concurrency control because we are optimistic and we don't lock any variable; we let every thread do its work thinking that it's going to work correctly and then check if it was correct. In practice, this allows for greater concurrency.

Let's start with the most obvious example, a bank account.

Let's write some code now, enter into the REPL and write:

```
(def account (ref 20000))
(dosync (ref-set account 10))
(deref account)
```

```
(defn test []
  (dotimes [n 5]
    (println n @account)
    (Thread/sleep 2000))
  (ref-set account 90))

(future (dosync (test)))
(Thread/sleep 1000)
(dosync (ref-set account 5))
```

Try to write the future and the `dosync` functions at the same time so you have the same results.

We have just three lines of code here but there are quite a few things happening.

First of all we define a `ref` (`account`); refs are the managed variables in transactions. They are also the first implementation we see of Clojure's identity idea. Note that the account is an identity now and it might take multiple values throughout its life.

We now modify its value, we do this within a transaction since refs cannot be modified outside of transactions; thus, the `dosync` block.

In the end, we print the account and we can use (`deref` account) or `@account`, as we did for promises and futures.

Refs can be read from anywhere, there is no need for it to be within a transaction.

Let's look at something a little bit more interesting now, write or copy the next code into the REPL:

```
(def account (ref 20000))

(defn test []
  (println "Transaction started")
  (dotimes [n 5]
    (println n @account)
    (Thread/sleep 2000))
  (ref-set account 90))

(future (dosync (test)))
(future (dosync (Thread/sleep 4000) (ref-set account 5)))
```

If everything goes well, you should have an output similar to the following screenshot:

```
clojure-concurrency.core=> (future (dosync (test)))
Transaction started
0 20000
#object[clojure.core$future_call$reify__6736 0x490bc5f4 {:status :pending, :val nil}]
clojure-concurrency.core=> (future (dosync (Thread/sleep 4000) (ref-set account 5)))
#object[clojure.core$future_call$reify__6736 0x2d31b139 {:status :pending, :val nil}]
clojure-concurrency.core=> 1 20000
2 20000
Transaction started
0 5
1 5
2 5
3 5
4 5
```

This might seem a little strange, what is happening?

The first transaction starts its process using the current value for account, the other transaction then modifies the value of account before the first transaction is finished; Clojure realizes this and it restarts the first transaction.

You shouldn't execute functions with side effects within transactions, as there is no guarantee that they will be executed only once. If you need to do something like that you should use an agent.

This is the first example of how a transaction works, but using ref-set is not a good idea in general.

Let's take a look at another example, the classic example of moving money from an account *A* to an account *B*:

```
(def account-a (ref 10000))
(def account-b (ref 2000))
(def started (clojure.core/promise))

(defn move [acc1 acc2 amount]
  (dosync
    (let [balance1 @acc1
          balance2 @acc2]
      (println "Transaction started")
      (clojure.core/deliver started true)
      (Thread/sleep 5000)
      (when (> balance1 amount)
```

```
        (alter acc1 - amount)
        (alter acc2 + amount))
      (println "Transaction finished"))))

(future (move account-a account-b 50))
@started
(dosync (ref-set account-a 20))
```

This is a better example of how transactions work; you will probably see something similar to the following screenshot:

```
clojure-concurrency.core=> (future (move account-a account-b 50))
#object[clojure.core$future_call$reify__6736 0x17f9691c {:status :pending, :val nil}]

Transaction started
clojure-concurrency.core=> @started
true
clojure-concurrency.core=> (dosync (ref-set account-a 20))
20
clojure-concurrency.core=>

clojure-concurrency.core=>
Transaction started

Transaction finished
```

First of all, you need to understand how the alter function works; it's simple and it receives:

- The ref that it has to modify
- The function that it has to apply
- The extra arguments

So this function:

```
(alter ref fun arg1 arg2)
```

Is translated to something like this:

```
(ref-set ref (fun @ref arg1 arg2))
```

This is the preferred way to modify the current value.

Let's see a step by step description of what's going on here:

1. We define two accounts with a balance of 10000 and 2000.
2. We try to move 500 units from the first account to the second but first we sleep for 5 seconds.
3. We announce (using the promise) that we have started the transaction. The current thread moves on, since it was waiting for the started value.
4. We set the balance of account-a to 20.
5. The first transaction realizes that something has changed and restarts.
6. The transaction goes on and is finished this time.
7. Nothing happens, since the new balance is not enough to move 50 units.

In the end, if you check the balance, like `[@account-a @account-b]`, you will see that the first account has 20 and the second account has 2000.

There is another use case that you should take into account; let's check the following code:

```
(def account (ref 1000))
(def secured (ref false))
(def started (promise))

(defn withdraw [account amount secured]
  (dosync
    (let [secured-value @secured]
      (deliver started true)
      (Thread/sleep 5000)
      (println :started)
      (when-not secured-value
        (alter account - amount))
      (println :finished))))

(future (withdraw account 500 secured))
@started
(dosync (ref-set secured true))
```

The idea is that if `secured` is set to true, you shouldn't be able to withdraw any money.

If you run it and then check for the value of `@account`, you'll see that even after changing the value of `secured` to true a withdrawal occurs. Why is that?

The reason is that transactions only check for values that you modify within a transaction or values that you read; here we are reading the secured value before the modification, so the transaction doesn't fail. We can tell the transaction to be a little bit more careful by using the following code:

```
(ensure secured)
;; instead of
@secured
```

```
(def account (ref 1000))
(def secured (ref false))
(def started (promise))

(defn withdraw [account amount secured]
  (dosync
    (let [secured-value (ensure secured)]
      (deliver started true)
      (Thread/sleep 5000)
      (println :started)
      (when-not secured-value
        (alter account - amount))
      (println :finished))))

(future (withdraw account 500 secured))
@started
(dosync (ref-set secured true))
```

Here almost the same thing happened. What is the difference?

There is one subtle difference, the second transaction can't finish until the first transaction is done. If you look at it in detail, you will notice that you can't modify the secured value until after the other transaction runs.

This is similar to a lock; not the best idea but useful in some cases.

Atoms

We have now seen how promises, futures, and transactions work in Clojure. We'll now see atoms.

Even though STM is very useful and powerful you'll see that in practice it is not very commonly used.

Atoms are one of Clojure's workhorses, when it comes to concurrent programming.

You can think of atoms as transactions that modify one single value. You might be thinking, what good is that? Imagine you had lots of events that you want to store in a single vector. If you are used to Java, you probably know that using a `java.util.ArrayList` package is bound to have problems; since, you are almost surely going to lose data.

In that case, you probably want to use a class from the `java.util.concurrent` package, how can you guarantee that you'll have no data loss in Clojure?

It's easy, atoms come to the rescue! Let's try this piece of code:

```
(clojure.core/use 'co.paralleluniverse.pulsar.core)
(def events (atom []))
(defn log-events [count event-id]
  (dotimes [_ count]
    (swap! events conj event-id)))
(dotimes [n 5]
  (spawn-fiber #(log-events 500 n)))
```

We are again using Pulsar and its lightweight threads. Here, we define an events atom and a `log-events` function.

The `log-events` execute a `swap!` a given number of times.

`Swap!` is similar to the `alter` function it receives:

- The atom that it should modify
- The function that it applies to the atom
- The extra arguments

In this case, it gives the atom the new value that comes from:

```
(conj events event-id)
```

We then spawn five fibers, each fiber adds 500 events to the events atom.

After running this, we can check for the number of events from each fiber like this:

```
(count (filter #(= 0 %) @events))
;; 500
(count (filter #(= 1 %) @events))
;; 500
(count (filter #(= 2 %) @events))
;; 500
(count (filter #(= 3 %) @events))
;; 500
(count (filter #(= 4 %) @events))
;; 500
```

As you can see, we have 500 elements from each fiber with no data loss and using Clojure's default data structures. There is no need to use special data structures for each use case, locks, or mutexes. This allows for greater concurrency.

When you modify an atom, you need to wait for the operation to be complete meaning it is synchronous.

Agents

What if you don't care about the result of some operation? You just need to fire something and then forget it. In that case agents are what you need.

Agents also run in separate thread pools, there are two functions that you can use to fire an agent:

- send: This executes your function in an implicit thread pool

- send-off: This tries to execute your function in a new thread but there's a change, it will reuse another thread

Agents are the way to go if you want to cause side effects in a transaction; since, they will only be executed after the transaction has completed successfully.

They work in a very simple manner, here is an example usage:

```
(def agt (agent 0))
(defn sum [& nums]
  (Thread/sleep 5000)
  (println :done)
  (apply + nums))
(send agt sum 10)  ;; You can replace send with send-off
                   ;; if you want this to be executed in a different
thread
@agt
```

If you copy and paste the exact previous code you will see a 0 and then a :done message, if you check for the value of @agt, then you will see the value 10.

Agents are a good way to execute a given task and modify some value in a different thread with simpler semantics than those of futures or manually modifying values in another thread.

Validators

We have seen the primary concurrency primitives now, let's see some utilities that apply to all of them at once.

We can define a validator that checks if the new value of some function is desirable or not; you can use them for refs, atoms, agents, and even vars.

The `validator` function must receive a single value and return true if the new value is valid or false otherwise.

Let's create a simple `validator` that checks if the new value is lower than 5:

```
(def v (atom 0))
(set-validator! v #(< % 5))
(swap! v + 10)

;; IllegalStateException Invalid reference state  clojure.lang.ARef.
validate (ARef.java:33)
```

We get an exception. The reason is that the new value (`10`) is not valid.

You can add 4 without a problem:

```
(swap! v + 4)
;; 4
```

Be careful with the validator and agents, since you will probably not know when an exception occurred:

```
(def v (agent 0))
(set-validator! v #(< % 5))
(swap! v + 10)
;; THERE IS NO EXCEPTION
```

Watchers

Similar to validators, there are also watchers. Watchers are functions that are executed whenever Clojure's identities get a new value. An important question is the thread in which watchers run. Watchers run in the same thread as the watched entity (if you add a watcher to an agent it will be run in the agent's thread), it will be run before the agent code executes, so you should be careful and use the old-value new-value instead of reading the value with `deref`:

```
(def v (atom 0))
(add-watch v :sample (fn [k i old-value new-value] (println (= i v) k
old-value new-value)))
(reset! v 5)
```

The `add-watch` function receives:

- The ref, atom, agent, or var that should be watched
- A key that will be passed to the watcher function
- A function with four parameters: the key, the reference itself, the old value, and the new value

After executing the previous code we get:

```
true :sample 0 5
```

core.async

The `core.async` is yet another way of programming concurrently; it uses the idea of lightweight threads and channels to communicate between them.

Why lightweight threads?

The lightweight threads are used in languages, such as go and Erlang. They excel in being able to run thousands of threads in a single process.

What is the difference between the lightweight threads and traditional threads?

The traditional threads need to reserve memory. This also takes some time. If you want to create a couple of thousand threads, you will be using a noticeable amount of memory for each thread; asking the kernel to do that also takes time.

What is the difference with lightweight threads? To have a couple of hundred lightweight threads, you only need to create a couple of threads. There is no need to reserve memory and lightweight threads are a mere software idea.

This can be achieved with most languages and Clojure is adding first class support (without changing the language this is part of the Lisp power) with using `core.async`! Let's have a look at how it works.

There are two concepts that you need to keep in mind:

- **Goblocks**: They are the lightweight threads.
- **Channels**: Channels are a way to communicate between goblocks, you can think of them as queues. Goblocks can publish a message to the channel and other goblocks can take a message from them. Just as there are integration patterns for queues, there are integration patterns for channels and you will find concepts similar to broadcasting, filtering, and mapping.

Now, let's play a little with each of them so you can understand better how to use them for our program.

Goblocks

You will find goblocks in the `clojure.core.async` namespace.

Goblocks are extremely easy to use, you need the go macro and you will do something similar to this:

```
(ns test
  (:require [clojure.core.async :refer [go]]))

(go
  (println "Running in a goblock!"))
```

They are similar to threads; you just need to remember that you can create goblocks freely. There can be thousands of running goblocks in a single JVM.

Channels

You can actually use anything you like to communicate between goblocks, but it is recommended that you use channels.

Channels have two main operations: putting and getting. Let's check how to do it:

```
(ns test
  (:require [clojure.core.async :refer [go chan >! <!]]))

(let [c (chan)]
  (go (println (str "The data in the channel is" (<! c))))
  (go (>! c 6)))
```

That's it!! It looks pretty simple, as you can see there are three main functions that we are using with channels:

- `chan`: This function creates a channel and the channels can store some messages in a buffer. If you want this functionality, you should just pass the size of the buffer to the `chan` function. If no size is specified, the channel can store only one message.

- `>!`: The put function must be used within a goblock; it receives a channel and the value you want to publish to it. This function blocks, if a channel's buffer is already full. It will block until something is consumed from the channel.

- `<!`: This takes function; this function must be used within a goblock. It receives the channel you are taking from. It is blocking and if you haven't published something in the channel it will park until there's data available.

There are lots of other functions that you can use with channels, for now let's add two related functions that you will probably use soon:

- `>!!`: The blocking put, works exactly the same as the `put` function; except it can be used from anywhere. Note that if a channel cannot take more data, this function will block the entire thread from where it runs.

- `<!!`: The blocking works exactly the same as the `take` function, except you can use this from anywhere and not just from inside goblocks. Just keep in mind that this blocks the thread where it runs until there's data available.

If you look into the `core.async` API docs (`http://clojure.github.io/core.async/`) you will find a fair amount of functions.

Some of them look similar to the functions that give you functionalities similar to queues, let's take a look at the `broadcast` function:

```
(ns test
  (:require [clojure.core.async.lab :refer [broadcast]]
            [clojure.core.async :refer [chan <! >!! go-loop]]))

(let [c1 (chan 5)
      c2 (chan 5)
      bc (broadcast c1 c2)]
  (go-loop []
    (println "Getting from the first channel" (<! c1))
    (recur))
  (go-loop []
    (println "Getting from the second channel" (<! C2))
    (recur))
  (>!! bc 5)
  (>!! bc 9))
```

With this you can publish it to several channels at the same time, this is helpful if you want to subscribe multiple processes to a single source of events with a great amount of separation of concern.

If you take a good look, you will also find familiar functions over there: `map`, `filter`, and `reduce`.

Depending on the version of core.async, some of these functions might not be there anymore.

Why are these functions there? Those functions are meant to modify collections of data, right?

The reason is that there has been a good amount of effort towards using channels as higher-level abstractions.

The idea is to see channels as collections of events, if you think of them that way it's easy to see that you can create a new channel by mapping every element of an old channel or you can create a new channel by filtering away some elements.

In recent versions of Clojure, the abstraction has become even more noticeable with transducers.

Transducers

Transducers are a way to separate the computations from the input source. Simply, they are a way to apply a sequence of steps to a sequence or a channel.

Let's look at an example of a sequence:

```
(let [odd-counts (comp (map count)
                       (filter odd?))
      vs [[1 2 3 4 5 6]
          [:a :c :d :e]
          [:test]]]
  (sequence odd-counts vs))
```

The comp feels similar to the threading macros, it composes functions and stores the steps of the computation.

The interesting part is that we can use the same odd-counts transformation with a channel, such as:

```
(let [odd-counts (comp (map count)
                       (filter odd?))
      input (chan)
      output (chan 5 odd-counts)]
  (go-loop []
    (let [x (<! output)]
      (println x))
      (recur)))
```

```
(>!! input [1 2 3 4 5 6])
(>!! input [:a :c :d :e])
(>!! input [:test]))
```

Summary

We have checked the core Clojure mechanisms for concurrent programming, as you can see, they feel natural and they build on already existing paradigms, such as immutability. The most important idea is what an identity and value is; we now know that we can have the following values as identifiers:

- Refs
- Atoms
- Agents

We can also get the snapshot of their value with the defer function or the @ shortcut.

If we want to use something a little more primitive, we can use promises or futures.

We have also seen how to use threads, or Pulsar's fibers. Most of Clojure's primitives aren't specific to some concurrency mechanism, so we can use any parallel programming mechanism with any type of Clojure primitive.

7
Macros in Clojure

In this chapter, we will get to know one of Clojure's most complicated facilities: macros. We will learn what they are for, how to write them, and how to use them. It can be a little challenging, but there is good news too. You should be aware of some tools from your knowledge of the Java language that can help you understand macros better. We will progress little by little with comparisons to other JVM languages, and in the end, we will write some macros and understand that we have been using them for a while.

We will learn about the following topics:

- Understanding Lisp's foundational ideas
- Macros as code modification tools
- Modifying code in Groovy
- Writing your first macro
- Debugging your first macro
- Macros in the real world

Lisp's foundational ideas

Lisp is a very different beast from what you used to know. According to Paul Graham, there are nine ideas that make Lisp different (these ideas have existed since the late 1950s), and they are:

1. Conditionals (remember, we are talking 1950s–1960s)
2. Functions as first-class citizens
3. Recursion
4. Dynamic typing
5. Garbage collection

6. Programs as sequences of expressions

7. The symbol type

8. Lisp's syntax

9. The whole language is there all the time: at compilation, runtime—always!

 If you can, read Paul Graham's essay *Revenge of the Nerds* (http://www.paulgraham.com/icad.html), where he talks about Lisp, what makes it different, and why the language is important.

These ideas have thrived even after the Lisp age; most of them are common nowadays (can you imagine a language without conditionals?). But the last couple of ideas are what makes us Lisp lovers love the syntax (we will fully understand what they mean through this chapter).

Common languages are trying to achieve the very same things now with a slightly different approach, and you, as a Java developer, have probably seen this.

Macros as code modification tools

One of the first and most common uses of macros is to be able to modify code; they work on the code level, as you will see. Why should we do that? Let's try to understand the problem with something that you are more familiar with—Java.

Modifying code in Java

Have you ever used AspectJ or Spring AOP? Have you ever had problems with tools such as ASM or Javassist?

You have probably used code modification in Java. It is common in Java EE applications, just not explicit. (Have you ever thought about what the @Transactional annotation does in Java EE or Spring applications?)

As developers, we try to automate everything we can, so how could we leave out our own devtools?

We have tried to create ways to modify the bytecode at runtime so that we don't have to remember to open and close resources, or so that we can decouple dependencies and get dependency injection.

If you use Spring, you probably know about the following use cases:

- The `@Transactional` annotation modifies the annotated method to ensure that your code is wrapped in a database transaction
- The `@Autowired` annotation looks for the required bean and injects it into the annotated property or method
- The `@Value` annotation looks for a configuration value and then injects it

You could probably think of several other annotations that modify the way your classes work.

The important thing here is that you understand why we want to modify code, and you probably already know a few mechanisms for doing it, including AspectJ and Spring AOP.

Let's take a look at how it is done in the Java world; this is what an aspect in Java looks like:

```
package macros.java;

public aspect SampleJavaAspect {
pointcutanyOperation() : execution(public * *.*(..));

    Object around() : anyOperation() {
System.out.println("We are about to execute this " +
thisJoinPointStaticPart.getSignature());
        Object ret = proceed();
        return ret;
    }
}
```

Aspects have the advantage that you can modify any code you like without having to touch it. This also has its drawbacks since you could modify the code in ways the original author didn't expect and thus cause bugs.

Another drawback is that you have an extremely limited field of action; you can wrap your modifications around some code or execute something before or after.

The libraries that generate this code are extremely complex and they can either create a proxy around your objects or modify the bytecode, at runtime or compile time.

As you can imagine, there are lots of things that you must be aware of, and anything could go wrong. Hence, debugging could prove complicated.

Modifying code in Groovy

Groovy has gone further down the road and it provides us with more solutions and more macro-like features.

Since Groovy 1.8, we have got a lot of AST transformations. What does AST stand for? It stands for **abstract syntax tree** — sounds complicated, right?

Before explaining it all, let's check what some of them do.

The @ToString annotation

The @ToString annotation generates a simple toString method that includes information about the class of the object and the value of its properties.

The @TupleConstructor annotation

The @TupleConstructor creates a constructor that is able to take all of the values of your class at once. Here is an example:

```
@TupleConstructor
class SampleData {
int size
   String color
boolean big
}

new SampleData(5, "red", false") // We didn't write this constructor
```

The @Slf4j annotation

The @Slf4j annotation adds an instance of a logger, called log by default, to your class, so you can do this:

```
log.info'hello world'
```

This can be done without having to manually declare the log instance, the class name, and so on. There are lots of other things that you can do with this type of annotation, but how do they work?

Now, what is AST and what does it have to do with Clojure macros? Come to think of it, it actually has a lot to do with them.

To answer that last question, you'll have to understand a little bit about how compilers work.

We all know that machines (your machine, the JVM, the Erlang BEAM machine) are not capable of understanding human code, so we need a process to convert whatever developers write into what machines understand.

One of the most important steps of the process is to create a syntax tree, something similar to the following figure:

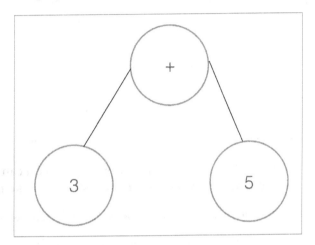

This is a very simple example of the following expression:

```
3 + 5
```

This tree is what we call the abstract syntax tree. Let's see the tree of something that's a bit more complicated, such as this piece of code:

```
if(a > 120) {
    a = a / 5
} else {
    a = 1200
}
```

Thus, the tree will look like the following figure:

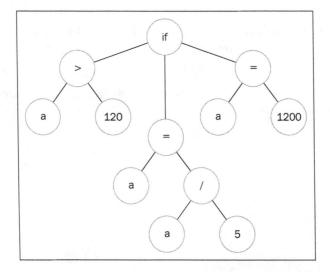

As you can see, the figure is still pretty straightforward, and you can probably understand how someone would execute code from a structure like this one.

Groovy's AST transformation is a way to meddle with such generated code.

As you can imagine, this is a much more powerful approach, but you are now messing with what the compiler generated; the probable downside to this is the complexity of the code.

Let's check, for instance, the code of the @Slf4j AST. It should be pretty simple, right? It just adds a log property:

```
        private Expression transformMethodCallExpression(Expressi
on exp) {
MethodCallExpressionmce = (MethodCallExpression) exp;
        if (!(mce.getObjectExpression()
instanceofVariableExpression)) {
            return exp;
        }
VariableExpressionvariableExpression = (VariableExpression) mce.
getObjectExpression();
        if (!variableExpression.getName().equals(logFieldName)
            || !(variableExpression.getAccessedVariable()
instanceofDynamicVariable)) {
            return exp;
```

```
        }
        String methodName = mce.getMethodAsString();
        if (methodName == null) return exp;
        if (usesSimpleMethodArgumentsOnly(mce)) return exp;

variableExpression.setAccessedVariable(logNode);

        if (!loggingStrategy.isLoggingMethod(methodName))
return exp;

        return loggingStrategy.wrapLoggingMethodCall(variableE
xpression, methodName, exp);
        }
```

 You can check the complete code at `https://github.com/groovy/` `groovy-core/blob/master/src/main/org/codehaus/groovy/` `transform/LogASTTransformation.java`, and it's also included with the code bundle of this chapter.

This doesn't look simple at all. It is just a fragment and still looks very complicated. What happens here is that you have to deal with the Java bytecode format and with compiler complications.

Here, we should remember point number 8 that Paul Graham made about the syntax of Lisp.

Let's write our last code example in Clojure:

```
(if (> a 120)
  (/ a 5)
  1200)
```

There's something peculiar about this piece of code: it feels very similar to the AST! This is not a coincidence. Actually, in Clojure and Lisp, you are directly writing the AST. This is one of the features that make Lisp a very simple language; you directly write what the computer understands. This might help you understand a little more about why code is data and data is code.

Imagine if you could modify the AST the same way that you modify any other data structure in your programs. But you can, and that's what macros are for!

Writing your first macro

Now that you have a clear understanding of how macros work and what they are for, let's start working with Clojure.

Let me present you with a challenge: write an `unless` function in Clojure, something that works like this:

```
(def a 150)

(my-if (> a 200)
  (println"Bigger than 200")
  (println"Smaller than 200"))
```

Let's give it a first try; maybe with something like the following syntax:

```
(defn my-if [cond positive negative]
  (if cond
    positive
    negative))
```

Do you know what would happen if you wrote this code and then ran it? If you test it, you will get the following result:

```
Bigger than 200
Smaller than 200
Nil
```

What's happening here? Let's modify it a bit so that we get a value and we can understand what's happening. Let's define it a bit differently, and let's return a value so that we see something different:

```
       (def a 500)
(my-if (> a 200)
  (do
    (println"Bigger than 200")
    :bigger)
  (do
    (println"Smaller than 200")
    :smaller))
```

We will get the following output:

```
Bigger than 200
Smaller than 200
:bigger
```

What's going on here?

When you pass parameters to a function, everything is evaluated before the actual code of the function runs, so over here, before the body of your function runs, you execute both of the `println` methods. After that, the `if` runs correctly and you get `:bigger`, but we still got an output for the positive and negative cases of our `if`. It looks like our code is not working!

How can we fix this? With our current tools, we probably need to write closures and change the `my-if` code to accept functions as parameters:

```
(defn my-if [cond positive negative]
  (if cond
    (positive)
    (negative)))

    (def a 500)
(my-if (> a 200)
  #(do
    (println"Bigger than 200")
    :bigger)
  #(do
    (println"Smaller than 200")
    :smaller))
```

This works, but there are several disadvantages:

- There are a lot of constraints now for the code (both clauses should now be functions)
- It doesn't work for every single case
- It is very complicated

In order to solve this problem, Clojure gives us macros. Let's have a look at how they work:

```
(defmacro my-if [test positive negative]
  (list 'if test positive negative))

(my-if (> a 200)
  (do
    (println"Bigger than 200")
    :bigger)
  (do
    (println"Smaller than 200")
    :smaller))
```

The output will be this:

```
;; Bigger than 200
;; :bigger
```

This is great! It works, but what just happened? Why did we just use a macro and why did it work?

 Macros are not normal Clojure functions; they are supposed to generate code and should return a Clojure form. This means that they should return a list that we can use as normal Clojure code.

Macros return code that will be executed later. And here is where point number nine of Paul Graham's list comes into play: you have all of the language all the time.

In C++, you have a mechanism called a macro; when you use it, you have a very limited set of things that you can do compared to actual C++ code.

In Clojure, you can manipulate the Clojure code any way you want, and you can use the full language here too! Since Clojure code is data, manipulating the code is as easy as manipulating any other data structure.

 Macros are run at compile time, which means that at the time of running the code, there is no trace of macros; every macro call is replaced with the generated code.

Debugging your first macro

Now, as you can imagine, since things can get complicated when using macros, there should be some way to debug them. We have two functions to accomplish that:

- `macroexpand`
- `macroexpand-1`

The difference between them has to do with recursive macros. There is no rule telling you that you can't use a macro from a macro (the whole language is there all the time, remember?). If you wish to go all the way through any macro, you can use `macroexpand`; if you wish to go a single step forward, you can use `macroexpand-1`.

Both of them show you the code generated by a macro call; this is what happens when you compile your Clojure code.

Give this a try:

```
(macroexpand-1
'(my-if (> a 200)
    (do
      (println"Bigger than 200")
      :bigger)
    (do
      (println"Smaller than 200")
      :smaller)))

;; (if (> a 200) (do (println"Bigger than 200") :bigger) (do
(println"Smaller than 200") :smaller))
```

There is not much more to macros than this; you now understand them to a good level of detail.

There are, however, many common problems that you will come across and tools for solving them that you should know about. Let's have a look.

Quote, syntax quote, and unquoting

As you can see, the my-if macro uses a quote in it:

```
(defmacro my-if [test positive negative]
  (list 'if test positive negative))
```

This happens because you need the if symbol as the first element in the resulting form.

Quoting is very common in macros, since we need to build code instead of evaluating it on the fly.

There is another type of quoting very common in macros — syntax quoting — that makes it easier to write code similar to the final code you want to generate. Let's change the implementation of our macro to this:

```
(defmacro my-if [test positive negative]
  '(if test positive negative))
```

```
(macroexpand-1
'(my-if (> a 200)
    (do
```

```
      (println"Bigger than 200")
      :bigger)
  (do
    (println"Smaller than 200")
    :smaller)))
```

```
;; (if clojure.core/test user/positive user/negative)
```

Let's see what happens here. For one, `(if test positive negative)` looks much more beautiful than the `list` function we had before, but the code generated with `macroexpand-1` looks pretty strange. What happened?

We just used a different form of quoting that allows us to quote full expressions. It does some interesting things. As you can see, it changes the parameters to fully qualified `var` names (`clojure.core/test`, `user/positive`, `user/negative`). This is something that you'll be grateful for in the future, but you don't need this for now.

What you need are the values of test, positive, and negative. How can you get them in this macro?

Using syntax quotes, you can ask for something to be evaluated inline with the unquote operator, like this:

```
(defmacro my-if [test positive negative]
  (if ~test ~positive ~negative))
```

Let's try our macro expansion again and see what we get:

```
user=> (defmacro my-if [test positive negative]
  #_=>    `(if ~test ~positive ~negative))
#'user/my-if
user=> (macroexpand-1
  #_=>    '(my-if (> a 200)
  #_=>        (do
  #_=>           (println "Bigger than 200")
  #_=>           :bigger)
  #_=>        (do
  #_=>           (println "Smaller than 200")
  #_=>           :smaller)))
(if (> a 200) (do (println "Bigger than 200") :bigger) (do (println "Smaller than 200") :smaller))
```

Unquote splicing

There are some other cases that become common in macros. Let's imagine we want to reimplement the > function as a macro and retain the ability to compare several numbers; what would that look like?

Maybe a first attempt could be something like this:

```
(defmacro>-macro [&params]
  '(> ~params))


(macroexpand'(>-macro 5 4 3))
```

The output of the preceding code is as follows:

```
user=> (defmacro >-macro [& params]
  #_=>    '(> ~params))
#'user/>-macro
user=>

user=> (macroexpand '(>-macro 5 4 3))
(clojure.core/> (5 4 3))
user=> (>-macro 5 4 3)
ClassCastException java.lang.Long cannot be cast to clojure.lang.IFn  user/eval1219 (form-init7702615529919007918.clj:1)
```

Do you see the problem here?

The problem is that we are trying to pass a list of values to `clojure.core/>` instead of passing the values themselves.

This is easily solved with something called **unquote splicing**. Unquote splicing takes a vector or list of parameters and expands it as if you had used the as parameter on a function or macro.

It works like this:

```
(defmacro>-macro [&params]
  '(> ~@params))  ;; In the end this works as if you had written
                  ;; (> 5 4 3)

(macroexpand'(>-macro 5 4 3))
```

The output of the preceding code is as follows:

```
user=> (defmacro >-macro [& params]
  #_=>     '(> ~@params)) ;; In the end this works as if you had written
#'user/>-macro
user=>                    ;; (> 5 4 3)

user=>

user=> (macroexpand '(>-macro 5 4 3))
(clojure.core/> 5 4 3)
user=> (>-macro 5 4 3)
true
```

You will use unquote splicing almost every time you have a variable number of arguments to a macro.

gensym

Generating code can be troublesome, and we end up discovering common issues.

See if you can find the issue in the following code:

```
(def a-var"hello world")

(defmacro error-macro [&params]
  '(let [a-var"bye world"]
     (println a-var)))

;; (macroexpand-1 '(error-macro))
;; (clojure.core/let [user/a-var user/"bye user/world"] (clojure.core/
println user/a-var))
```

This is a common issue when generating code. You overwrite another value, Clojure doesn't even let you run this, and it displays something like the following screenshot:

```
user=> (def a-var "hello world")
#'user/a-var
user=> (defmacro error-macro [& params]
  #_=>     '(let [a-var "bye world"]
  #_=>        (println a-var)))
#'user/error-macro
user=> (macroexpand-1 '(error-macro))
(clojure.core/let [user/a-var "bye world"] (clojure.core/println user/a-var))
user=> (error-macro)

CompilerException java.lang.RuntimeException: Can't let qualified name: user/a-var, compiling:(/private/var/folders/4s/yxd1cnqn17dd30b_z4b2
7kyw0000gn/T/form-init7702615529919007918.clj:1:1)
```

But don't worry; there's another way in which you can make sure you are not messing with your environment, which is the gensym function:

```
(defmacro error-macro [&params]
  (let [a-var-name (gensym'a-var)]
    `(let [~a-var-name "bye world"]
       (println ~a-var-name))))
```

The gensym function creates a new var-name each time the macro is run, which guarantees that there is no other var-name that it obscures. If you try the macro expansion now, you will get this:

```
(clojure.core/let [a-var922"bye world"] (clojure.core/println
a-var922))
```

The following screenshot is the result of the preceding code:

```
user=> (def a-var "hello world")
#'user/a-var
user=> (defmacro error-macro [& params]
  #_=>    (let [a-var-name (gensym 'a-var)]
  #_=>      `(let [~a-var-name "bye world"]
  #_=>         (println ~a-var-name))))
#'user/error-macro
user=> (macroexpand-1 '(error-macro))
(clojure.core/let [a-var1274 "bye world"] (clojure.core/println a-var1274))
user=> (error-
error-handler    error-macro     error-mode
user=> (error-m
error-macro    error-mode
user=> (error-macro)
bye world
nil
```

Macros in the real world

Do you want to know when it is that macros are used extensively? Think about defn; what's more, do this:

```
(macroexpand-1 '(defn sample [a] (println a)))

;; (def sample (clojure.core/fn ([a] (println a))))
```

Did you know that defn is a macro in clojure.core that creates a function and binds it to a var in the current namespace?

Clojure is filled with macros; if you want some samples, you can look at Clojure core, but what else can you do with macros?

Let's have a look at some interesting libraries:

- yesql: The yesql library is a very interesting sample of code generation. It reads SQL code from a SQL file and generates the Clojure functions accordingly. Look for the defquery and defqueries macros in the yesql project on GitHub; it can be very enlightening.

- core.async: If you are familiar with the go language and goroutines, you would probably like to have that same functionality in the Clojure language. This isn't necessary since you could have provided them yourself! The core.async library is just goroutines for Clojure, and it is provided as a library (no obscure language change is needed). This shows a great example of the power of macros.

- core.typed: With macros, you can even change the dynamic nature of Lisp. The core.typed library is an effort that allows you to define type constraints for your Clojure code; macros are extensively used here to generate boilerplate code and checks. This is probably much more complex.

References

If you need further references, you can look at the following list. There are entire books committed to the topic of macros. I recommend two in particular:

- Mastering Clojure Macros (https://pragprog.com/book/cjclojure/mastering-clojure-macros).
- Let over Lambda (http://letoverlambda.com/).It talks about common Lisp, but the knowledge is very valuable.

Summary

You now understand the power of macros and have a very strong grasp of how they work, but we just touched the tip of the iceberg when it comes to macros.

In this chapter, we learned about the following:

- Fundamentals of how macros work
- Modifying your code in Groovy
- The relation of macros to other tools in the Java world
- Writing your own macros

I am sure you've enjoyed working with Clojure so far, and moving forward, I'd recommend you to keep reading and exploring this amazing language.

Index

Symbols

A

C

D

Thank you for buying
Clojure for Java Developers

About Packt Publishing

Packt, pronounced 'packed', published its first book, *Mastering phpMyAdmin for Effective MySQL Management*, in April 2004, and subsequently continued to specialize in publishing highly focused books on specific technologies and solutions.

Our books and publications share the experiences of your fellow IT professionals in adapting and customizing today's systems, applications, and frameworks. Our solution-based books give you the knowledge and power to customize the software and technologies you're using to get the job done. Packt books are more specific and less general than the IT books you have seen in the past. Our unique business model allows us to bring you more focused information, giving you more of what you need to know, and less of what you don't.

Packt is a modern yet unique publishing company that focuses on producing quality, cutting-edge books for communities of developers, administrators, and newbies alike. For more information, please visit our website at www.packtpub.com.

About Packt Open Source

In 2010, Packt launched two new brands, Packt Open Source and Packt Enterprise, in order to continue its focus on specialization. This book is part of the Packt Open Source brand, home to books published on software built around open source licenses, and offering information to anybody from advanced developers to budding web designers. The Open Source brand also runs Packt's Open Source Royalty Scheme, by which Packt gives a royalty to each open source project about whose software a book is sold.

Writing for Packt

We welcome all inquiries from people who are interested in authoring. Book proposals should be sent to author@packtpub.com. If your book idea is still at an early stage and you would like to discuss it first before writing a formal book proposal, then please contact us; one of our commissioning editors will get in touch with you.

We're not just looking for published authors; if you have strong technical skills but no writing experience, our experienced editors can help you develop a writing career, or simply get some additional reward for your expertise.

Clojure Reactive Programming

ISBN: 978-1-78398-666-8   Paperback: 232 pages

Design and implement highly reusable reactive applications by integrating different frameworks with Clojure

1. Learn how to leverage the features of functional reactive programming using Clojure.

2. Create dataflow-based systems that are the building blocks of reactive programming.

3. Learn different Functional Reactive Programming frameworks and techniques by implementing real-world examples.

Clojure Web Development Essentials

ISBN: 978-1-78439-222-2   Paperback: 232 pages

Develop your own web application with the effective use of the Clojure programming language

1. Use Clojure to create robust, ready-to-be deployed web applications.

2. Get to grips with Clojure through successive implementation of applications using new features.

3. Explore the in-depth concepts of Clojure, such as templating, request routing, input validation, and database transactions, and utilize Java interoperability.

Please check **www.PacktPub.com** for information on our titles

[PACKT] open source
community experience distilled
PUBLISHING

Clojure Data Analysis Cookbook

Second Edition

ISBN: 978-1-78439-029-7   Paperback: 372 pages

Dive into data analysis with Clojure through over 100 practical recipes for every stage of the analysis and collection process

1. Take control of your data, from collection to classification.

2. Troubleshoot and solve data analysis problems using Clojure and a variety of Java libraries.

3. Get clear, practical techniques for every stage of data analysis.

Mastering Clojure Data Analysis

ISBN: 978-1-78328-413-9   Paperback: 340 pages

Leverage the power and flexibility of Clojure through this practical guide to data analysis

1. Explore the concept of data analysis using established scientific methods combined with the powerful Clojure language.

2. Master Naïve Bayesian Classification, Benford's Law, and much more in Clojure.

3. Learn with the help of examples drawn from exciting, real-world data.

Please check **www.PacktPub.com** for information on our titles

www.ingramcontent.com/pod-product-compliance
Lightning Source LLC
Chambersburg PA
CBHW060145060326
40690CB00018B/3982